GET STARTED

Foundations in English

James R. Morgan

Nancy Douglas

NATIONAL GEOGRAPHIC
LEARNING

Australia · Brazil · Mexico · Singapore · United Kingdom · United States

Get Started, Foundations in English
Nancy Douglas, Author
James R. Morgan, Author

Publisher: Sherrise Roehr

Executive Editor: Sarah Kenney

Senior Development Editor: Margarita Matte

Assistant Editor: Becky Long

Media Researcher: Leila Hishmeh

Director of Global Marketing: Ian Martin

Senior Product Marketing Manager:
   Caitlin Thomas

Sr. Director, ELT & World Languages:
   Michael Burggren

Production Manager: Daisy Sosa

Content Project Managers: Beth Houston

Senior Print Buyer: Mary Beth Hennebury

Composition: MPS Limited

Cover/Text Design: Brenda Carmichael

Art Director: Brenda Carmichael

Cover Image: © Jimmy Chin

Inside Front Cover Image: MIKEY SCHAEFER/
   National Geographic Creative

For product information and technology assistance, contact us at
Cengage Learning Customer & Sales Support, cengage.com/contact
For permission to use material from this text or product,
submit all requests online at **cengage.com/permissions**
Further permissions questions can be emailed to
permissionrequest@cengage.com

Get Started ISBN: 978-1-305-94929-4

Get Started + Audio CD ISBN: 978-1-337-62117-5

National Geographic Learning
20 Channel Center Street
Boston, MA 02210
USA

National Geographic Learning, a Cengage Learning Company, has a mission to bring the world to the classroom and the classroom to life. With our English language programs, students learn about their world by experiencing it. Through our partnerships with National Geographic and TED Talks, they develop the language and skills they need to be successful global citizens and leaders.

Locate your local office at **international.cengage.com/region**

Visit National Geographic Learning online at **NGL.Cengage.com/ELT**
Visit our corporate website at **www.cengage.com**

Printed in China
Print Number: 04   Print Year: 2019

Photo Credits

SCOPE & SEQUENCE

	Unit Goals	Vocabulary	Grammar	Listening	Speaking
UNIT 1 **CLASSROOM INSTRUCTIONS** p. 2	Follow classroom instructions; Greet people; Ask someone to repeat	answer, ask, circle, listen, read, say	The imperative: *Open your book. Look at the picture.*	Listen to match instructions to actions	*Good morning. Can you repeat that?* **please, yes / no, Numbers 1-5**
UNIT 2 **MY NAME IS...** p. 8	Spell names; Meet someone; Say your name	The alphabet	Subject pronouns: (*I, you, he, she*); Simple present: *be* **Mr., Ms.**	Listen to spelling of words Listen for contractions	*Hi. I'm... It's nice to meet you.* **Can you spell that?**
UNIT 3 **OUR CLASSROOM** p. 14	Identify classroom objects; Ask to use something; Say thank you	backpack, computer, dictionary, pen, phone	Singular and plural nouns; Subject pronouns: (*it, they*); *this / these* **ID card**	Listen for contractions	*Can I use your... / Sure. Thanks. / You're welcome.* **scissors**

PUT IT TOGETHER 1 The Simple Present: *Yes / No* Questions and short answers with *be*; Review of Units 1-3 p. 20

	Unit Goals	Vocabulary	Grammar	Listening	Speaking
UNIT 4 **PERSONAL INFORMATION** p. 24	Ask for and give personal information; Identify ownership; Talk on the phone	Numbers 1-20 and zero; email address, phone number, student ID number **@, .com, .edu**	Subject pronoun: *we*; Possessive adjectives: *my, your, his / her its, our, your, their*; **(best) friend**	Listen for email addresses, ID numbers, and telephone numbers	*Excuse me, who's calling? Hi, Amy. It's Ray.* **different, new, sorry, yeah**
UNIT 5 **MY NEIGHBORHOOD** p. 30	Talk about places in your neighborhood; Get someone's attention; Ask for and give directions	bank, park, restaurant, school, store **favorite**	There is / There are **street, car, parking garage, tree**	Listen to follow directions on a map	*Excuse me. Is there a / an __ around here? Go straight. Turn right / left.* **drugstore, library**
UNIT 6 **COUNTRIES** p. 36	Say countries and nationalities; Ask where someone is from; Describe your city	China / Chinese, Peru / Peruvian Turkey / Turkish **flag, language, soup**	be + adjective; be + adjective + noun **interesting, famous, fun, food, actor, beautiful, big/ small, exciting, old**	Listen for countries and nationalities; Listen for sentence stress	*Where are you from? I'm from... My city is famous for its parks.* **near**

PUT IT TOGETHER 2 The Simple Present: *Wh-* Questions with *be*; Review of Units 4-6 p. 42

	Unit Goals	Vocabulary	Grammar	Listening	Speaking
UNIT 7 **FAMILY** p. 46	Talk about your family; Describe appearance; Ask about age	grandfather, mother (mom), (older / younger) sister, cousin, parents	The Simple Present: *have* (affirmative only) **Numbers 21-40, free time, homework, husband**	Listen and identify people in a photo	*You look like your brother / sister.* *How old are you? / I'm 21.* **on vacation, wife**
UNIT 8 **MY FAVORITES** p. 52	Describe movies, TV shows and music; Talk about likes and dislikes	funny, popular, scary, hip-hop, pop, rock **band / group, singer, song**	The Simple Present: *like* and other verbs (affirmative and negative) **play video games, read comic books, watch movies**	Listen for pronunciaiton of verbs ending in -s / -es	*Do you like...?* *Yeah, it's OK.* *No, not really.*
UNIT 9 **TIME** p. 58	Tell time; Talk about your schedule; Make and reply to a suggestion	art, English, history, math, What time is it? / It's 3:10	Questions with *when*; Responses with: *at, in, before, after, now, later, today, tomorrow* **morning, afternoon, evening, reservation, test, drama club, swim practice**	Listen and complete a class schedule	*Let's study for the test together. / (That) sounds good.* *Are you free in the morning? / No, I have class.*
PUT IT TOGETHER 3 The Simple Present: *Yes / No* Questions and Short Answers; Review of Units 7-9 p. 64					
UNIT 10 **MY ROUTINE** p. 68	Describe your daily schedule; Explain how often things happen; Talk about your weekend	get up, take a shower, go to school, do homework **routine**	Adverbs of frequency **choose** **early** **late** **miss (class)** **nervous**	Listen for how frequently something happens	*What do you usually do on the weekend? / Not much. I…*
UNIT 11 **IMPORTANT DAYS** p. 74	Say the date; Talk about special days and what people do; Say you know or don't know something	Months of the year (January, February…); Ordinal numbers (first, second…)	The Simple Present: *Wh-* questions with verbs other than *be* **What do you do?, check in, buy, serve, wear, have a party, New Year's Day / Eve**	Listen and write the date	*When is the Halloween party? I'm not sure. / I don't know.* **film / food festival, last, spring, summer, fall, winter**
UNIT 12 **FOOD** p. 80	Talk about your favorite foods; Order and pay for food and drinks	*soup and salad, chicken and rice, ice cream, tea* **breakfast, lunch, dinner, dessert, eat, drink, milk, soda, water, delicious, good**	Partitives (*a cup of, a slice of*) and *some* **healthy, hungry, snack**	Listen to identify foods	*I'd like the chicken sandwich, (please). /* *Anything else? /* *A bag of chips, (please).* *That's $6.50.*
PUT IT TOGETHER 4 Review of all Question Forms; Review of Units 10-12 p. 86					

Workbook p. 90   Activities p. 102   Vocabulary List p. 106

1 CLASSROOM INSTRUCTIONS

1 VOCABULARY

A 🔊 **Track 2** Listen and repeat.

listen

say

read

write

ask

answer

circle

cover

open

close

look

repeat

B Work with a partner.

1. Cover each row of words on page 2 with a paper.

2. Point 👆 to a picture. Use a word in the box.

answer	ask	circle	close	cover	listen
look	open	read	repeat	say	write

C Work with a partner.

Write the words from **B**.

Put the papers on the desk.

D Work with another pair. Play the game. Use all the words.

Take a paper.

In 1 minute, draw the word.
Your partner says the word.

Correct (✓) word = 1 point
To win, get the most points.

2 GRAMMAR

A **A** 🔊 **Track 3** Look at the pictures. Listen and repeat.

book

conversation

teacher

page

name

picture

question

Listen and repeat.

sentence

English

word

B Study the chart.

The Imperative					
Look *at*		picture.	Open		book.
Read		sentence.	Close		book.
Say		word.	Ask	your	teacher.
Circle	the	word.	Write		name.
Cover		page.	Listen	and	repeat.
Listen *to*		conversation.	**Notice!** look <u>at</u>, listen <u>to</u>		
Answer		question.			

C 🔊 **Track 4** Match the sentences from **B** under the pictures. Listen and check your answers.

1.

Answer the question.

2.

_____

3.

_____

4. _____

5. _____

6. _____

7. _____

8. _____

9. _____

10. _____

11. _____

12. _____

D 🔄 Work with a partner. Cover **A–C**. Write the missing words.

and	the	your

1. Listen to _____**the**_____ conversation.

2. Write _____ name.

3. Close _____ book.

4. Answer _____ question.

5. Say _____ word.

6. Circle _____ word.

7. Listen _____ repeat.

8. Read _____ sentence.

9. Open _____ book.

10. Cover _____ page.

11. Look at _____ picture.

12. Ask _____ teacher.

E 🔷 Work in a group. Go to page 102. Play a game. **Student A** says a sentence to **Student B**. **Student B** says a sentence to **Student C**. Say the sentence again, and again. **Student E** says the sentence.

3 SPEAKING

A Say the words and sentences in the Useful Language box with the teacher.

Useful Language		
Numbers 1–5	Greet people	Ask someone to repeat
1 one 2 two 3 three 4 four 5 five	Good morning. Good afternoon. Good evening.	Can you repeat that? Can you say that again?

B 🔊 Track 5 Read and listen to the conversation.

► WORD BANK
yes
no
please

TEACHER: Good morning, everyone. Please open your books to page five.

STUDENT: Emily?

TEACHER: Yes?

STUDENT: Can you repeat that?

TEACHER: Yes. Open to page five.

C Work with a partner. Say the conversation in **B**.

D Track 6 Listen. Circle the words.

1. **TEACHER INSTRUCTOR:** Good morning / afternoon, everyone. Please open your books to page 2 / 3 / 4.

   STUDENT: Emily? Can you repeat that / say that again?
   Yes, open to page 2 / 3 / 4.

2. **TEACHER INSTRUCTOR:** Good morning / afternoon, everyone. Please open your books to page 3 / 4 / 5.

   STUDENT: Emily? Can you repeat that / say that again?

   TEACHER INSTRUCTOR: Yes, open to page 3 / 4 / 5.

E Work with a partner. Say the conversations in **D**.

F Write five actions.

Examples: _____Close your book.   Write your name.   Repeat: 1, 3, 5.   Say "Good morning."_____

1. _____

2. _____

3. _____

4. _____

5. _____

G Work in a group of four.

1. Say an action from **F**.

2. Students **A–C** do the action.

3. Circle correct (✓) or incorrect (✗) for students 1–3.

Please write your name.

Can you repeat that, Rosa?

Yes, write...

	Action 1		Action 2		Action 3		Action 4		Action 5	
Student 1	✓	✗	✓	✗	✓	✗	✓	✗	✓	✗
Student 2	✓	✗	✓	✗	✓	✗	✓	✗	✓	✗
Student 3	✓	✗	✓	✗	✓	✗	✓	✗	✓	✗

2 MY NAME IS...

1 VOCABULARY

A 🔊 Track 7 **PRONUNCIATION** Listen and repeat.

B 🔁 Work with a partner.
STUDENT 1: Say letters A–M.
STUDENT 2: Say letters N–Z.

C 🔁 Repeat **B**. Change roles.

Letters of the Alphabet

Aa	Bb	Cc	Dd
Ee	Ff	Gg	Hh
Ii	Jj	Kk	Ll
Mm	Nn	Oo	Pp
Qq	Rr	Ss	Tt
Uu	Vv	Ww	Xx
Yy	Zz		

D 🔊 **Track 8** Look at the picture.
Listen to the names 1–5.
Write the letters.

1. ___ ___ ___ r ___

2. ___ ___ h ___ ___ ___

3. L ___ ___ ___

4. ___ a ___ ___ ___

5. ___ l ___ ___ ___ a

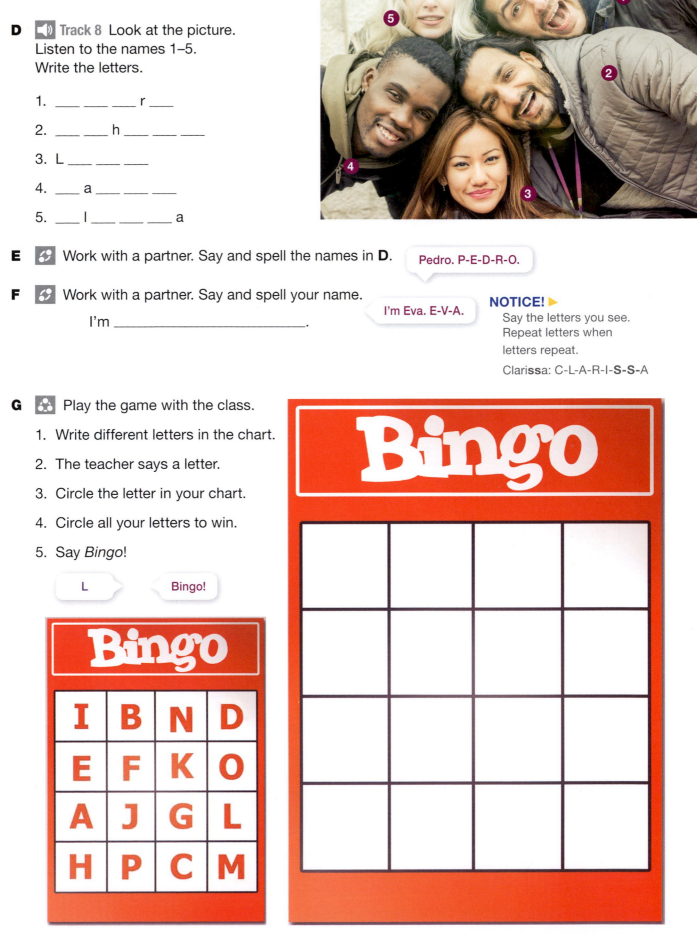

E 🗣 Work with a partner. Say and spell the names in **D**.

> Pedro. P-E-D-R-O.

F 🗣 Work with a partner. Say and spell your name.

I'm _____ .

> I'm Eva. E-V-A.

NOTICE! ▶
Say the letters you see.
Repeat letters when
letters repeat.

Clari**ss**a: C-L-A-R-I-**S-S**-A

G 🎲 Play the game with the class.

1. Write different letters in the chart.

2. The teacher says a letter.

3. Circle the letter in your chart.

4. Circle all your letters to win.

5. Say *Bingo*!

> L

> Bingo!

Bingo

I	B	N	D
E	F	K	O
A	J	G	L
H	P	C	M

Bingo

My Name Is… **9**

2 GRAMMAR

A Look at the pictures. Say the words.

B Study the chart.

Subject Pronouns: *I, you, he, she* / The Simple Present: *be*			
I'm	a	student.	*Be* has three forms: *am*, *are*, and *is*.
You're			*I am = I'm you are = you're he is = he's she is = she's*
He's		teacher.	Use *I'm / you're / he's / she's* in conversation.
She's			

C 🔊 Track 9 Look at the pictures. Listen and repeat.

1.

   a. I am a student.
   b. I'm a student.

2.

   a. You are a teacher.
   b. You're a teacher.

3.

   a. He is a soccer player.
   b. He's a soccer player.

4.

   a. She is a doctor.
   b. She's a doctor.

5.

   a. He is a businessman.
   b. He's a businessman.

6.

   a. She is a programmer.
   b. She's a programmer.

D 🔊 Track 10 Listen again. Circle the sentences in **C**.

E Write the missing words.

1. Ms. Yao __is__ a teacher.

2. James _____ a programmer.

3. I _____ a soccer player.

4. Mary _____ a businesswoman.

5. You _____ a student.

6. Mr. Lopez _____ a doctor.

F Rewrite the sentences from **E**.

1. She's a teacher.

2. _____

3. _____

4. _____

5. _____

6. _____

G 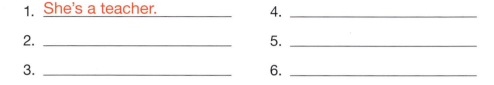 Write names in the chart. Tell a partner. Say it two ways.

Job	Name
a soccer player	
a teacher	
a businessman / businesswoman	

Ms. Sato is a teacher.
She's a teacher.

H Work in a group. Play the game. Take turns.

3 SPEAKING

A Say the sentences in the Useful Language box with the teacher.

Useful Language		
Greet someone	**Say your name**	**Meet someone**
Hello. / Hi.	I'm… / My name is…	(It's) nice to meet you. (It's) nice to meet you, too.

B Track 11 Read and listen to the conversation.

LISA: Hello. I'm Lisa.

TOMAS: Hi, Lisa. My name is Tomas.

LISA: Nice to meet you.

TOMAS: Nice to meet you, too.

C Work with a partner. Say the conversation in **B**.

D Work with a partner. Say the conversation. Use your names.

E Cover the Useful Language box and the conversation in **B**. Read the conversations below. Guess the words.

1. A: _____. My name _____ Aya.

   B: _____, Aya. _____ Leo.

   A: Nice to meet _____.

   B: Nice to meet _____, too.

2. A: _____, _____ Marc.

   B: _____, Marc. _____ Paula.

   A: Nice to meet _____.

   B: _____, too.

F 🔊 Track 12 Listen. Write the words in **E**.

G 🔄 Work with a partner. Say the conversations in **E**.

H 👥 Meet six classmates. Write their names below.

My classmates	
1. _____	4. _____
2. _____	5. _____
3. _____	6. _____

A: Hi, I'm Jun.

B: Hi, Jun. My name is Sofia.

A: Can you spell that, please?

B: S-O-F-I-A.

A: Nice to meet you, Sofia!

▶ **WORD BANK**

Ask for spelling

Can you spell that?

I 🔄 Work with a partner. Say a sentence about a classmate in **H**. Point to the person.

She's Sofia, and he's…

3 OUR CLASSROOM

1 VOCABULARY

a. **backpack**
b. **door**
c. **(white)board**
d. **chair**
e. **pen**
f. **clock**
g. **(laptop) computer**
h. **notebook**
i. **desk**
j. **dictionary**
k. **bookcase**
l. **eraser**
m. **map**
n. **screen**
o. **table**
p. **textbook**
q. **pencil**
r. **phone**
s. **umbrella**
t. **window**

A 🔊 **Track 13** Look at the pictures. Listen and say the words.

B Write the letters.

1. p_e_ _n_
2. n___t___b___ ___k
3. ch___i___
4. ___en___ ___l
5. ___ack___ack

6. ___ ___ one
7. dic___ ___ ___ ___ar___
8. ___ ___aser
9. c___mp___te___
10. ta___l___

C 🔁 Work with a partner. Say and spell the words in **B**.

D 🔁 Cover the word list. Look at the picture.
STUDENT A: Say the words for a–j.
STUDENT B: Say the words for k–t.

E 🔁 Repeat **D**. Change roles.

F Look at the word list. Circle the things in your classroom. Then draw a picture of your classroom.

G 🔁 Give your picture to a partner. Your partner points to things in the picture and says them.

2 GRAMMAR

A Look at the pictures. Say the words.

B Study the chart.

NOTICE!▶ it is = *it's*   they are = *they're*   what is = *what's*

Subject Pronouns: *it* and *they* / Singular and Plural Nouns / *this* and *these*	**What's this?**				
		It's	a	pencil.	Use *a* / *an* after *it's*.
			an	eraser.	Use *an* before a vowel (*a, e, i, o, u*).
	What are these?				
		They're		pencils.	Don't use *a* / *an* after *they're*.
				erasers.	Add *-s* for two or more. (*pencils, erasers*)

C Write the other form.

1. they are = ___they're___

2. _____ = she's

3. it is = _____

4. _____ = I'm

5. _____ = you're

6. he is = _____

7. _____ = what's

NOTICE!▶ *this* = one thing
these = two or more

D 🔊 Track 14 **PRONUNCIATION Contractions with *is*.** Listen and repeat.

1. What's this?   It's a backpack.

2. What is this?   It is a backpack.

NOTICE!▶ What**'s** this?   What **is** this?
It**'s** a pen.   It **is** a pen.

E 🔊 Track 15 Listen. Circle your answers.

1. What's this? / What is this?

    It's a map.

2. What's this?

    It's a bookcase. / It is a bookcase.

3. What's this?

    It's a textbook. / It is a textbook.

4. What's this? / What is this?

    It's a laptop.

F 🔲 Work with a partner. Ask and answer the questions in **E**.

G 🔁 Write the missing words. Ask your partner the questions.

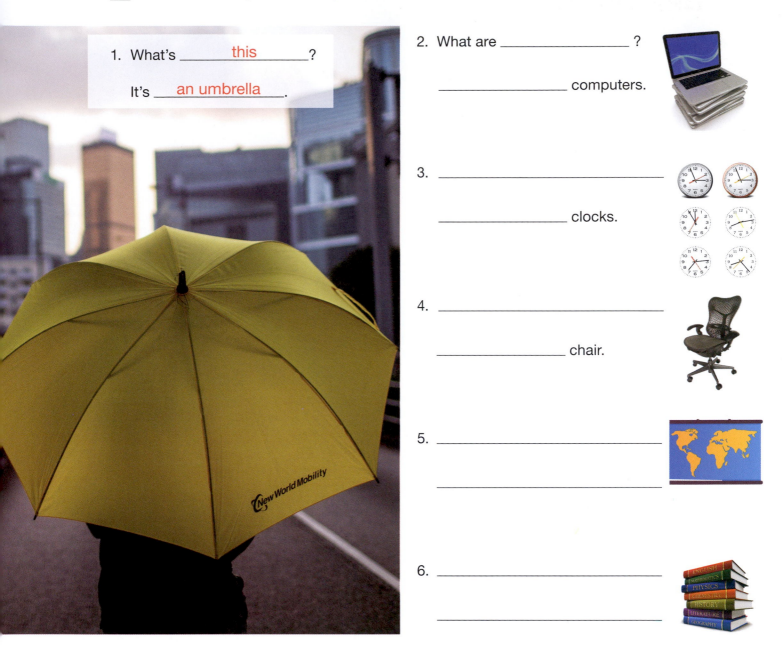

1. What's ___this___?

   It's ___an umbrella___.

2. What are _____ ?

   _____ computers.

3. _____

   _____ clocks.

4. _____

   _____ chair.

5. _____

   _____

6. _____

   _____

H 🔁 Work with a partner. Correct the sentences together.

1. What's these?

   They're notebooks.

2. What's this?

   It's a ID card.

3. What are these?

   They're are notebooks.

4. What's this?

   Is a phone.

▶ **WORD BANK**
ID card

I 👥 Work in groups of four. Play the game.

   STUDENT A: Show an item or items from your backpack. Ask, *What's this? / What are these?*

   STUDENTS B-D: Say the item(s). Correct answer = 1 point.

3 SPEAKING

Useful Language	
Ask to use something	**Say thank you and reply**

Can I use your _____?
   Sure. (= *yes*)
	Thank you. / Thanks.
	   You're welcome. / No problem.

A Say the sentences in the Useful Language box with the teacher.

B 🔊 Track 16 Read and listen to the conversation.

PAULA: Can I use your pen?

OMAR: Sure.

PAULA: Thanks.

OMAR: You're welcome.

C 🔄 Say the conversation in **B**.

D Cover the Useful Language box and the conversation in **B**. Read the conversations below. Guess the words.

1. A: Can I use your pen?

   B: Sure.

   A: _____ you.

   B: You'_____ welcome.

2. A: Can I use your pen?

   B: Sure.

   A: _____ .

   B: _____ problem.

E 🔊 Track 17 Listen. Write the words in **D**.

F 🔁 Say the conversations in **D**.

G 🔁 Look at the pictures. Ask and answer the questions.

What's this?

It's...

What are these?

They're...

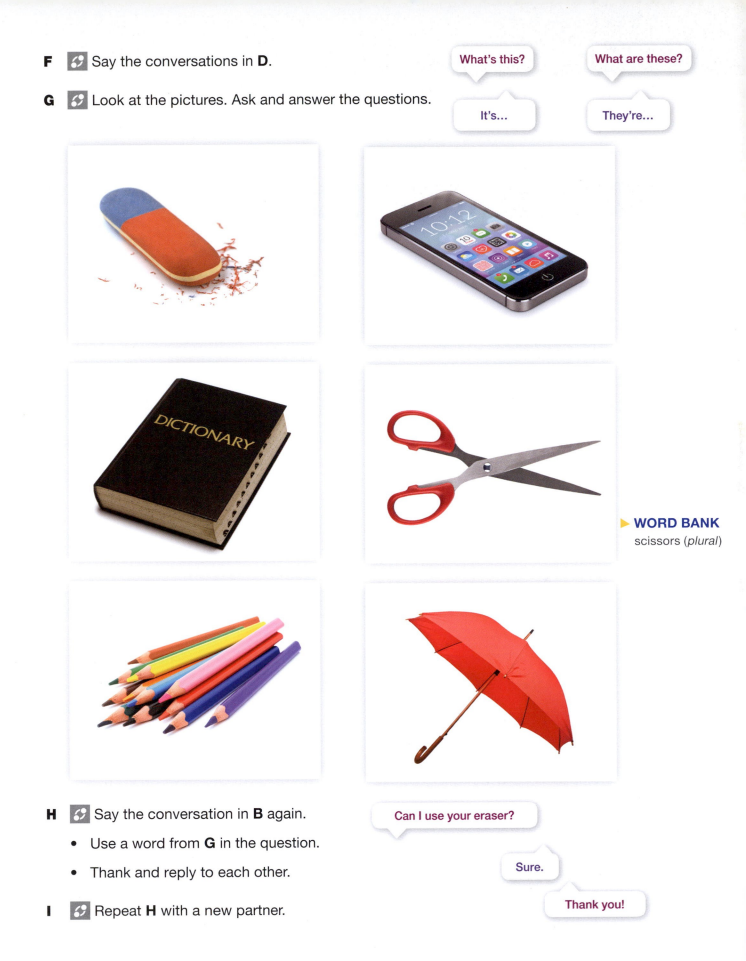

▶ **WORD BANK**
scissors (*plural*)

H 🔁 Say the conversation in **B** again.

- Use a word from **G** in the question.
- Thank and reply to each other.

I 🔁 Repeat **H** with a new partner.

Can I use your eraser?

Sure.

Thank you!

1 GRAMMAR

A Study the chart.

Statements			Yes / No Questions			In questions, *am / is / are* comes first.
You	are	a student.	**Are**	**you**	a student**?**	Use "." at the end of statements.
She	is	a student.	**Is**	**she**	a student**?**	Use "?" at the end of questions.
They	are	students.	**Are**	**they**	students**?**	

B Write questions.

1. I'm in this class. ⟶ Am I in this class? _____

2. You're a teacher. ⟶ _____

3. He's a teacher. ⟶ _____

4. She's a programmer. ⟶ _____

5. It's an eraser. ⟶ _____

6. They're at home. ⟶ _____

C Follow the pattern. Write statements and questions.

A	B	C	D	E	F
are	he	are	a	English	student(s)
is	they	is	an	student	teacher

1. (**B, C, D, E**) He is a student. _____

2. (**B, C, D, E, F**) _____

3. (**B, C, F**) _____

4. (**A, B, D, E**) _____

5. (**A, B, D, E, F**) _____

6. (**A, B, F**) _____

D 🔊 **Track 18** Listen. Write the missing words.

▶ **WORD BANK**
I don't know.

1. **A:** What's this?

   B: I don't know. _____ laptop?

2. A: _____ she _____ teacher?

   B: I don't know. Maybe.

3. A: What are these?

   B: I don't know. _____ maps?

E Study the chart.

Yes / No Questions			Answers	
Am	I	in this class?	**Yes, you are.**	**No, you're not.**
Are	you	a student?	**Yes, I am.**	**No, I'm not.**
Is	he she	a student?	**Yes, he is.** **Yes, she is.**	**No, he's not.** **No, she's not.**
Is	it	her name?	**Yes, it is.**	**No, it's not.**
Are	they	students?	**Yes, they are.**	**No, they're not.**

F Read the questions. Circle the answers.

1. Are you a student?   a. Yes, I'm.   b. Yes, I am.

2. Is your name Carlos?   a. Yes, he is.   b. Yes, it is.

3. Is she a programmer?   a. No, she's not.   b. No, she is.

4. Is Mr. Green a teacher?   a. Yes, she is.   b. Yes, he is.

5. Are you a teacher?   a. No, I'm not.   b. No, you're not.

6. Are Jan and Tom students?   a. Yes, she is.   b. Yes, they are.

NOTICE! ▶
Don't use contractions (*I'm, you're, he's, they're*) in *Yes* answers.

G Look at the pictures. Write the missing words.

1. Is _____ a backpack?

   Yes, _____ is.

2. _____ phones?

   No, _____ .

3. _____ businessman?

   No, _____ .

4. _____ ?

   _____ .

2 SEE IT AND SAY IT

A Look at the picture. Find the 15 (fifteen) people and things. Write the words.

programmer _____ _____ _____ _____

_____ _____ _____ _____ _____

_____ _____ _____ _____ _____

B Work with a partner. Point to something in the picture. Ask questions about things. Practice spelling. Take turns.

       A: What's this?

       B: It's a clock.

       A: Can you spell that?

       B: Sure. It's C-L-O-C-K.

3 LISTENING

A Read the conversations. Guess the answers.

CONVERSATION 1

A: Hi, I'm Alex.

B: Hi, Alex. _____ name is Hector.

A: Hector. Can you spell _____ , please?

B: Sure. It's H-E-C-T-O-R.

A: Oh, OK. Got it. Nice to meet you, Hector.

B: Nice to meet _____ , too!

CONVERSATION 2

A: Can I use _____ phone?

B: Sure, no problem.

A: Thank you!

B: _____ welcome.

CONVERSATION 3

A: _____ morning, class.

B: _____ morning, Mr. Lee.

A: Please _____ your books. OK, listen and repeat.

   "What's _____ ?"

B: "What's this?"

B 🔊 Track 19 Listen. Check your answers in **A**.

C ✂ Cover the conversations in **A**. Choose a picture. Write your own conversation.

D 👥 Say your conversation for another pair.

4 CROSSWORD PUZZLE

A Complete the puzzle. Go to page 103.

4 PERSONAL INFORMATION

1 VOCABULARY

A 🔊 Track 20 Listen. Say the numbers.

B 🔁 Work with a partner. Circle the words (*zero*, *one*, *two*...) in the puzzle.

0 zero	
1 one	11 eleven
2 two	12 twelve
3 three	13 thirteen
4 four	14 fourteen
5 five	15 fifteen
6 six	16 sixteen
7 seven	17 seventeen
8 eight	18 eighteen
9 nine	19 nineteen
10 ten	20 twenty

G	C	S	I	X	T	E	E	N	T	E	N
C	T	H	I	R	T	E	E	N	I	N	E
S	J	F	S	E	V	E	N	T	E	E	N
E	T	I	Z	I	F	U	S	E	V	E	N
I	W	V	E	K	O	L	I	A	O	N	E
G	E	E	R	F	U	H	E	F	Z	G	J
H	L	F	O	U	R	T	L	I	G	N	T
T	V	S	E	R	T	W	E	F	H	R	H
E	E	R	S	O	E	O	V	T	X	G	R
E	E	N	I	N	E	T	E	E	N	H	E
N	L	G	X	R	N	T	N	E	L	X	E
Y	E	I	G	H	T	W	E	N	T	Y	W

WORD BANK
@ = at
.com = dot com
.edu = dot e-d-u
.net = dot net

NOTICE! ▶
We often say *oh* (not *zero*)
with phone numbers.

C 🔊 Track 21 Look at the chart. Listen to Dmitry.

Student Name	Student ID Number	✉ Email Address	📱 Phone Number
Dmitry Kozlov	07-12-20	DmitryK@zmail.com	290-4346
Amelia Ortiz	04-____-____	Amelia____@linkmail____	____-____14
Max Tran	____-____-____	Max____@starlink ____	____-____
Leah Yu	____-____-____	LeahYu@CCF____	____-____

D 🔊 Track 22 Listen. Complete the chart in **C**.

E 🔄 Work with a partner.

- Point 👆 to a student in **C**.

- Say the information.

> This is Dmitry. Student ID Number: 07, 12, 20. Email address…

F Write your email address and phone number.

Email: _____

Phone: _____

G 🔗 Ask five classmates for an email address and phone number. Write the information in your notebook.

> What's your email address?

> What's your phone number?

> It's…

> It's…

A Study the chart.

Subject Pronoun	Example	Possessive Adjective	Example
I	I'm Pablo.	my	My name is Pablo.
you	You're a student.	your	Your ID number is 32-71-02.
he	He's a businessman.	his	His phone number is 555-2436.
she	She's a doctor.	her	Her email address is doc12@zmail.com.
it	It's a cat.	its	Its name is Maru.
we	We're students.	our	This is our class.
you	You're students.	your	Ms. Cho is your teacher.
they	They're teachers.	their	This is their class.

Red words come before *am / is / are.* Blue words come before words like *name, ID number, class,* and *teacher.*

◄ **Notice!** It's a cat. Its name is Maru.

B Cover the chart in **A**. Match the words.

I'm Pablo.
My name is Pablo.

_C_ 1. I   a. your

____ 2. you   b. its

____ 3. he   c. my

____ 4. she   d. their

____ 5. it   e. our

____ 6. we   f. his

____ 7. you   g. her

____ 8. they

C Underline the words that are blue in **A**.

1. She's <u>our</u> teacher.

2. His ID number is 07-11-18.

3. Your teachers are here.

4. I say my name.

5. What's your phone number?

6. Is he your friend?

7. Is her phone number 443-0121?

8. Their class is in Room 105.

9. They're my classmates.

10. Its home is near here.

► **WORD BANK**
friend

D Write the missing words.

1. ___Her___ name is Clara.

2. ___She___'s a student.

3. _____ email address is clara.ar@zmail.com.

4. _____ _____ programmer.

5. _____ phone number _____ 555-1212.

6. _____ _____ is Justin.

7. _____ a family.

8. _____ last name _____ Smith.

9. Emily Soams is 20. _____ my best friend.

10. _____ students.

11. _____ class _____ in Room 5.

E Think of a person. Write the information.

First name		Last name	
Phone number		Email address	

F  Tell a partner. My best friend is Antonio. His last name is…

G Get into small groups. Play the game.

These are your glasses.

And this is her pen.

3 SPEAKING

A Say the words and sentences in the Useful Language box with the teacher.

Useful Language	Answer the phone Identify yourself	Hello? Hi, _____. It's...
	Ask who someone is on the phone	Excuse me, who's calling?

B 🔊 Track 23 Read and listen to the conversation.

LEO: Hello?

MAX: Hi, Leo.

LEO: Uh, hi. Excuse me, who's calling?

MAX: It's Max.

LEO: Oh, hi Max! Sorry! Your phone number is different.

MAX: Yeah, it's new. It's now 697-8075.

▶ **WORD BANK**
different
new
Sorry!
Yeah = Yes

C 🔄 Work with a partner. Say the conversation in **B**.

D Cover the Useful Language box in **A** and the conversation in **B**. Read the conversations below. Guess the words.

1. A: _____?

   B: Hi, Ryan.

   A: Uh, hi. Excuse me, _____ calling?

   B: _____ Tony.

   A: Oh, hi Tony! Sorry! Your phone number is different.

   B: Yeah. It's now _____.

2. A: _____?

   B: Hi, Sofia.

   A: Uh, hi. Excuse me, _____ calling?

   B: It's Emma, _____ classmate.

   A: Oh, hi Emma! Your number isn't in my phone. Is it _____?

   B: Yeah.

E 🔊 **Track 24** Listen. Write the words and the phone numbers.

F 🔄 Work with a partner. Say the conversations in **D**.

G Think of a new name and phone number.

Name: _____

Phone number: _____

H 🔄 Sit back-to-back with a partner.
Say the conversation in **B** again.

    STUDENT A: Answer the phone. Write the caller's name and phone number.

    STUDENT B: Use your name and phone number from **G**.

Caller: _____

Phone number: _____

I 🔄 Change roles. Repeat **H**.

J 🔄 Repeat **H** and **I** with a different partner.

Hello?

Hi, So-Hyun.

Hi. Uh, excuse me, who's calling?

It's your classmate...

5 MY NEIGHBORHOOD

1 VOCABULARY

Places in a neighborhood

1. ATM
2. bank
3. bus stop
4. cafe / coffee shop
5. gym
6. (movie) theater
7. park
8. post office
9. restaurant
10. school
11. store
12. supermarket

▶ **WORD BANK**
- clothing store
- bookstore
- department store

This is a neighborhood in San Francisco.

A 🔊 Track 25 Listen and repeat.

B Write the words.

1. rapk   _park_
2. ygm   _____
3. oolsch   _____
4. nbak   _____

5. otsp ceioff _____
6. usb otsp   _____
7. treos   _____
8. aunratrets   _____

9. TMA   _____
10. ecaf   _____
11. eatthre _____
12. persuketmar _____

C 🔁 Work with a partner.

1. Cover the word list.

2. Ask and answer the question.

> What's this?

> It's a bank.

D 🔊 Track 26 Listen to the phone calls. Circle the answer.

1. Maria is at _____.
   a. home   b. school   c. a coffee shop

2. Jon is at the _____.
   a. restaurant   b. bus stop   c. ATM

3. Marc is at _____.
   a. school
   b. the movie theater
   c. the bookstore

E 🔁 Say your ideas. Use two places from the word list.

My favorite _____ is _____.

> My favorite store is Uniqlo.

▶ **WORD BANK**
favorite

2 GRAMMAR

A Look at the pictures. Say the words.

a tree   two trees   some trees   no trees

B Study the chart.

There is / There are				
There	is	a / an	bus stop / ATM	on my street.
	are	some	stores	
		no	parks	in my neighborhood.
		three	cafes	

► **WORD BANK**
street

C Circle the answers.

NOTICE!►
there's = there is

1. There's / There are a clothing store near here.

2. There's / There are some good restaurants in my city.

3. In my neighborhood, there's / there are two cafes. My favorite is Coco's.

4. There's / There are no stores on my street.

5. There's / There are one department store on Main Street.

D 🔁 Correct the sentences.

1. There are no park.

    There are no parks.

2. There's restaurant.

_____

3. There are not gyms.

_____

4. There're some banks.

_____

5. There are a three cafes.

_____

6. There's two supermarkets.

_____

E 🔊 **Track 27** Look at the picture. Listen and read.

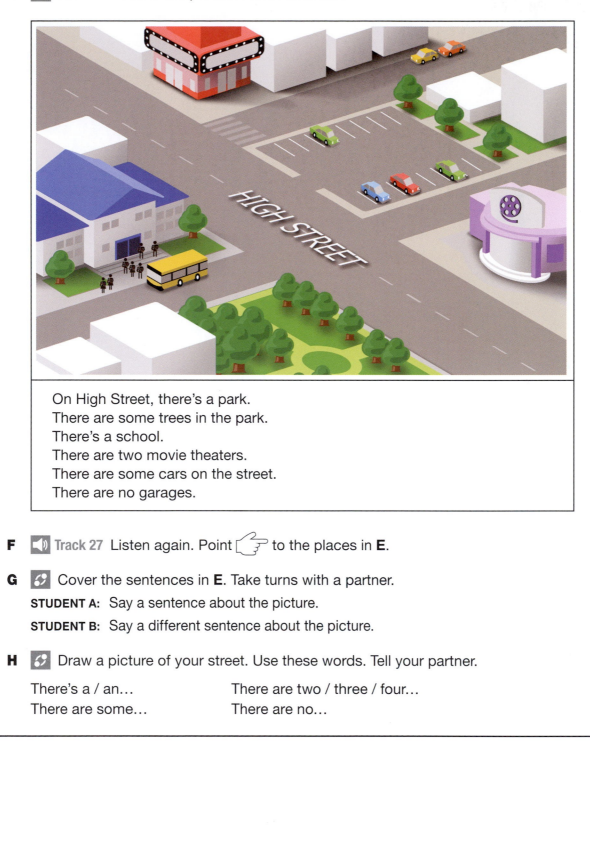

On High Street, there's a park.
There are some trees in the park.
There's a school.
There are two movie theaters.
There are some cars on the street.
There are no garages.

F 🔊 **Track 27** Listen again. Point 👉 to the places in **E**.

G 🔄 Cover the sentences in **E**. Take turns with a partner.

STUDENT A: Say a sentence about the picture.

STUDENT B: Say a different sentence about the picture.

H 🔄 Draw a picture of your street. Use these words. Tell your partner.

There's a / an…   There are two / three / four…
There are some…   There are no…

3 SPEAKING

A Say the sentences in the Useful Language box with the teacher.

Useful Language	Get someone's attention	Excuse me?
	Ask for directions	Is there a(n)… around here?
	Give directions	Go straight. Turn left / right on Jay Street. The ATM is on the left / right. Sorry, I don't know.

B 🔊 Track 28 Read and listen to the conversation.

WOMAN: Excuse me?

MAN: Yes?

WOMAN: Is there an ATM around here?

MAN: Yeah. Go straight and turn right on Jay Street.
The ATM is on the left.

WOMAN: Great, thanks!

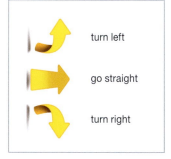

turn left

go straight

turn right

C Where is the ATM? Circle the number.

D 🔁 Say the conversation in **B**.

E 🔊 Track 29 Where are the six places? Listen. Write the number of each place (1–6) on the map.

1. subway station 🚇   **3.** bookstore   **5.** gas station ⛽

2. supermarket   **4.** coffee shop   **6.** post office

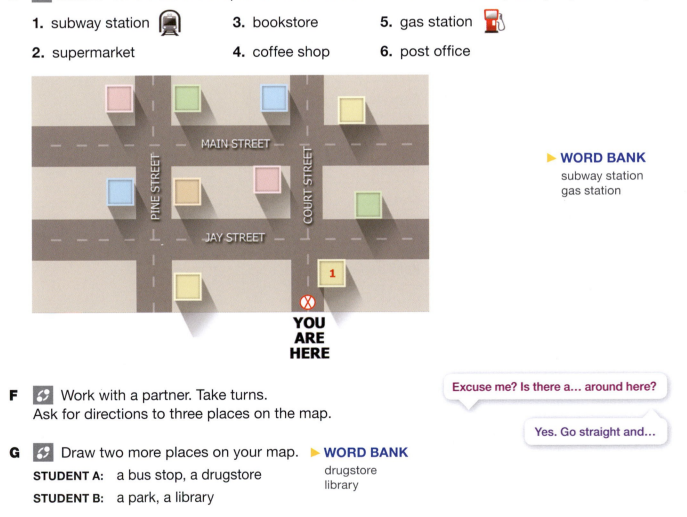

▶ **WORD BANK**
subway station
gas station

F 🔁 Work with a partner. Take turns.
Ask for directions to three places on the map.

> Excuse me? Is there a... around here?

> Yes. Go straight and...

G 🔁 Draw two more places on your map. ▶ **WORD BANK**

STUDENT A: a bus stop, a drugstore   drugstore
STUDENT B: a park, a library   library

H 🔁 Ask for directions to the places on your partner's map. Draw them on your map.

> Excuse me? Is there a bus stop around here?

6 COUNTRIES

1 VOCABULARY

	Country	Nationality
	China	Chinese
	Japan	Japanese
	Portugal	Portuguese
	Vietnam	Vietnamese
	Australia	Australian
	Brazil	Brazilian
	Peru	Peruvian
	Canada	Canadian
	Korea	Korean
	Mexico	Mexican
	The United States	American
	Venezuela	Venezuelan
	The United Kingdom	British
	Spain	Spanish
	Turkey	Turkish
	Sweden	Swedish

Copacabana Beach and Ipanema beach in Rio de Janeiro, Brazil

A 🔊 **Track 30** Listen and say the countries and nationalities.

B 🔄 Work with a partner.

- Cover the nationalities in the chart.

- Take turns: Say a country. Then say the nationality.

C Complete the sentences. Use words from the chart.

1. The 2020 Olympic Games are in _____.

2. Canberra is a city in _____.

3. English and French are the two main languages in _____.

4. There are over a billion (1,000,000,000) people in _____.

5. Pho is the name of a _____ soup.

6. Wales is a country in _____.

7. _____ is a country in Europe and Asia.

8. Soccer player Cristiano Ronaldo is _____.

9. This is the _____ flag:

10. Chichen Itza is in _____.

D 🔊 **Track 31** Listen and check your answers in **C**.

E 🔄 Work with a partner. Write three sentences.
Use the sentences in **C** as a model.

F 🔷 Work with another pair. Say your sentences in **E**.
(Do not say the country or nationality.) The other
pair guesses.

NOTICE! ▶
in + city, country
<u>in</u> Beijing
<u>in</u> China

▶ **WORD BANK**
flag
France – French
language
soup

Pho

Ruins of Chichen Itza in Mexico

2 GRAMMAR

A Look at the pictures. Say the words.

► WORD BANK
interesting

beautiful | exciting | old | big ↔ small

B Study the chart.

Be + adjective			
New York	is	interesting.	Words like *big*, *small*, and *interesting* come after *am*, *is*, and *are*.
The neighborhoods	are		

C Write the missing letters.

1. __ nt __ r __ st __ ng

2. __ ld

3. b __ g

4. __ xc __ t __ ng

5. sm __ ll

6. b __ __ __ t __ f __ l

D Complete the sentences.
Then match 1, 2, and 3 with a picture.

► WORD BANK
famous
fun

1. It's int _eresting_ .

   It'_s_ in Russia.

   The subway stations _____ beautiful.

2. It _____ exciting.

   The parties _____ fun.

   It's _____ Brazil.

3. _____ in England.

   There _____ a clock.

   It's fam_____. It's o_____.

London
_____

Rio de Janeiro
_____

Moscow
_____

E Study the chart.

Be + adjective + noun					
New York	is	an	interesting	city.	Words like *big*, *small*, and *interesting* also come before nouns (words like *city*, *neighborhoods*, *park*, and *car*).
There	are			neighborhoods.	

F 🔊 **Track 32 PRONUNCIATION** Listen and repeat.

1. There are **two Mexican restaurants** near here.

2. **Venice** is my **favorite city**.

3. **Kimchee** is a **Korean food**.

4. He's a **famous actor**.

▶ **WORD BANK**
food
actor

G Rewrite the sentences. Add the new words.

1. There are some neighborhoods in Los Angeles.

   (interesting) _____ There are some interesting neighborhoods in Los Angeles. _____

2. She's a teacher. (English) _____

3. It's my phone. (new) _____

4. Lima is a city. (big) _____

5. They're her pictures. (beautiful) _____

6. There are no buildings. (old) _____

7. There's a restaurant on my street. (famous) _____

8. Ibiza is an island. (Spanish) _____

H 👥 Work with a partner. Think of a place. Write 3–4 sentences about the place. Use words like *big, fun, interesting*.

It's in Orlando, Florida. _____
It's a fun and exciting place. _____
It's a famous theme park. _____

Is it Disney World?

I 👥 Join another pair. Say your sentences. Your partners guess.

Is it Disney World?

Humble Administrator's Garden in Suzhou, China

3 SPEAKING

A Say the sentences in the Useful Language box with the teacher.

Useful Language	
Ask where someone is from	**Describe your city**

Where are you from?
  (I'm from) China.
Where in China?
  (I'm from) Suzhou. It's near Shanghai.
	My city is famous for its parks.
	New York City is famous for Central Park.

B 🔊 Track 33 Read and listen to the conversation.

MEI: Where are you from, Luis?

LUIS: The Dominican Republic. And you?

MEI: I'm from China.

LUIS: Oh? Where in China?

MEI: Suzhou. It's a city near Shanghai. It's famous for its beautiful parks.

▶ **WORD BANK**
near

C 🔄 Work with a partner. Answer the questions.

1. Where is Luis from?

2. Where is Mei from?

3. Her city is famous for something. What?

D Work with a partner. Say the conversation in **B**.

E Complete the sentences.

1. I'm from _____.

2. It's famous for _____.

> I'm from Buenos Aires. It's famous for its exciting nightlife!

F Say the conversation in **B** again. Use your ideas in **E**.

G Read the name in the chart. Where is the man from? Write his country and nationality.

Famous person	Country / Nationality	City
Justin Bieber		*London (Ontario)*
1.		
2.		
3.		
4.		

H Complete the chart in **G**. Use your phone to help you.

1. Write the names of four famous people from different countries.

2. Write the person's country and nationality.

3. Write the city the person is from.

I Work in a group. Play the game. Take turns.

1. Choose a person in your chart.

2. Ask your partners: *Where is… from?*

3. The first person with the correct answer gets 1 point.

4. Then ask him or her: *Where in…?*

5. A correct answer gets 1 point.

> Where is Justin Bieber from?

> He's American!

> No, sorry.

> He's from Canada!

> Yes. Where in Canada?

> Ontario?

1 GRAMMAR

A Study the chart.

NOTICE!▶ Both answers are OK.
What is it? It's an ATM. / An ATM.

Yes / No Question		Is	it	a	computer?	Yes, it is. / No, it's not.
Wh- Question	What	is	it?			(It's) a computer.
Yes / No Question		Are	they	in	Lima?	Yes, they are. / No, they're not.
Wh- Question	Where	are	they?			(They're) in Lima.
Yes / No Question		Is	she	your	friend?	Yes, she is. / No, she's not.
Wh- Question	Who	is	she?			(She's) my friend.

In *Wh-* questions, words like *what*, *where*, and *who* come first.

B 🔊 Track 34 **PRONUNCIATION** Read the sentences. Then listen and repeat.

Yes / No Questions (↗)	1. Is it a computer?	2. Are they in Lima?	3. Is she your friend?
Wh- Questions (↘)	1. What is it?	2. Where are they?	3. Who is she?

C Match the questions and answers.

___b___ 1. Where are you now?   a. He's my friend.

_____ 2. What's your email address?   b. ~~I'm at home.~~

_____ 3. Who are you with?   c. At school.

_____ 4. Where's your school?   d. Tomas.

_____ 5. What's a tablet?   e. It's suzy@zmail.com.

_____ 6. Who's Tomas?   f. It's in my neighborhood.   ▶ **WORD BANK**
job

_____ 7. Where are they?   g. It's a computer.

_____ 8. What's your job?   h. I'm a programmer.

D Follow the pattern. Write questions.

A	B	C	D	E
where	is	the students	nickname	class
what	are	your	teacher	Lola
who			in	Mr. West

1. (**A, B, C**) <u>Where are the students?</u>

2. (**A, B, C**) _____

3. (**A, B, C, D**) _____

4. (**A, B, C, D**) _____

5. (**A, B, C, D**) _____

6. (**B, C, D, E**) _____

7. (**B, C, D, E**) _____

8 (**B, C, D, E**) _____

E 🔄 Work with a partner. Ask and answer the questions in **D**.

F 🔊 Track 35 Complete the questions. Then listen and check your answers.

CELIA: Hey, Lynn. It's nice to see you. _____ your friend?

LYNN: Celia, this is Anong. She's our new classmate.

CELIA: Hi, Anong. _____ you from?

ANONG: I'm from Thailand.

CELIA: _____ from Bangkok?

ANONG: No, I'm not. I'm from a small city, Chiang Rai. _____, Celia?

CELIA: I'm from Brazil.

ANONG: _____ in Brazil?

CELIA: From São Paulo.

ANONG: Well, it's nice to meet you, Celia. Hey, _____ our class in Room 15?

LYNN: No, today it's in Room 10.

ANONG: OK. _____ our teacher?

LYNN: Ms. Lopez.

ANONG: OK, thanks. Bye.

CELIA & LYNN: Bye, Anong.

G Think of a new name. Write the information in your notebook.

Your new name	Nationality	Country	City
Ian	Australian	Australia	Sydney

H 👥 Work in groups of three. Use the information in G. Write a new conversation.

Kate, this is Ian. He's our new classmate.

Hi, Ian. Where are you from?

Dubai airport terminal

FLIGHT	FROM	STATUS
12	LA PAZ	ON TIME
17	SHANGHAI	ON TIME
19	MEXICO CITY	ON TIME
15	HANOI	ON TIME
2	LOS ANGELES	ON TIME
18	HANOI	ON TIME
11	MEXICO CITY	ON TIME
20	LOS ANGELES	ON TIME
6	STOCKHOLM	ON TIME
9	MEXICO CITY	ON TIME

2 SEE IT AND SAY IT

A Look at the information. Use *there is / there are* and the words in the box. Write sentences.

a	no	one	some	two

▶ **WORD BANK**
flight

1. (La Paz) **There's a flight from La Paz.**

2. (Shanghai) _____

3. (Mexico City) _____

4. (Berlin) _____

5. (Los Angeles) _____

6. (Stockholm) _____

7. (Hanoi) _____

8. (Istanbul) _____

B 🔁 Complete the chart. Use the model. Say sentences about cities and people.

City	Country	Nationality
La Paz	Bolivia	
Shanghai		Chinese
Mexico City		
Berlin		German
Los Angeles		
Stockholm	Sweden	
Hanoi	Vietnam	
Istanbul	Turkey	

> La Paz is in Bolivia.
> A person from
> Bolivia is...

C Choose a city in **B**. Write four sentences about it in your notebook. Use these words.

| beautiful | big | exciting | famous for | fun | interesting | old | small |

D 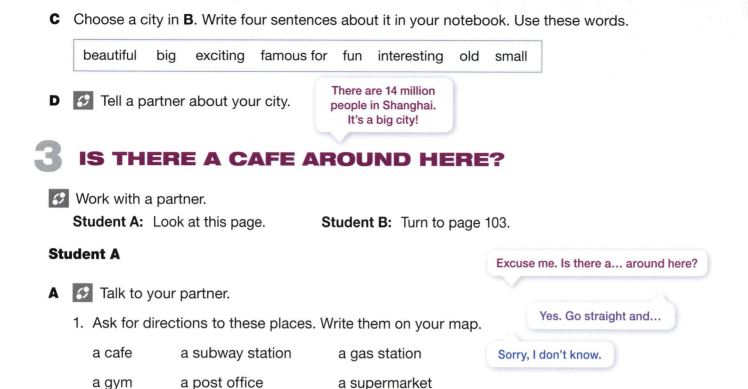 Tell a partner about your city.

> There are 14 million people in Shanghai. It's a big city!

3 IS THERE A CAFE AROUND HERE?

Work with a partner.

Student A: Look at this page.   **Student B:** Turn to page 103.

Student A

A Talk to your partner.

> Excuse me. Is there a... around here?

> Yes. Go straight and...

> Sorry, I don't know.

1. Ask for directions to these places. Write them on your map.

   a cafe   a subway station   a gas station

   a gym   a post office   a supermarket

2. Two places above are NOT on your map. When your partner says *Sorry, I don't know*, write an X on the words.

B Look at your map. Listen and give your partner directions. When a place is not on your map, say *Sorry, I don't know.*

C Check answers with your partner. Are the places on your map correct?

1 VOCABULARY

Zoe's Family

1. **grandmother**
2. **grandfather**
3. **mother (mom)**
4. **father (dad)**
5. **older sister**
6. **younger brother**
7. **aunt**
8. **uncle**
9. **cousin**
10. **grandparents**
11. **parents**

A 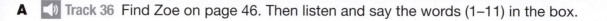 🔊 **Track 36** Find Zoe on page 46. Then listen and say the words (1–11) in the box.

NOTICE!▶

B Complete the sentences about Zoe's family.

Dylan is **Zoe's** brother.
Dylan is **her** brother.

1. Dylan is Zoe's ___brother___.

2. Paul is her _____.

3. Marisa is her _____.

4. Teresa is her _____.

5. Oscar is her _____.

6. Diana is her _____.

7. Lucas is her _____.

8. Stefani is her _____.

9. Kevin is her _____.

10. Paul and Teresa are her _____.

11. Kevin and Diana are her _____.

C 🔁 Work with a partner. Look at the pictures on page 46.

- Cover the word list and your answers in **B**.

- Say a sentence about each person in Zoe's family.

> Dylan is her younger brother.
> Marisa is her...

D 🔁 Work with a partner. Complete each sentence.

1. These are my _____.	2. This is my _____.	3. This is me with my _____ and _____.
a. brothers	a. dad	a. mom, cousin
b. parents	b. grandmother	b. grandfather, dad
c. sisters	c. younger sister	c. aunt, uncle

E Find three photos of family members. Write a sentence about each photo in your notebook.

F 🔁 Work with a partner. Show and talk about your photos.

> This is my baby cousin, Bella!

G 🔁 Repeat **F** with a different partner.

2 GRAMMAR

A Study the pictures and the chart.

a big family

short / long hair

a lot of friends

Have		
I / You	have	a big family.
He / She / It	has	short / long hair.
We / They	have	a lot of friends.

B Circle the correct words.

1. I always (has / (have)) fun in class.

2. Mr. Angelo (has / have) a big family.

3. My friends (has / have) a lot of free time.

4. Her sister (has / have) a new car.

5. Our mother (has / have) an exciting job.

6. They (has / have) five children.

7. My cousin (has / have) long hair.

8. The students (has / have) a lot of homework.

▶ **WORD BANK**
free time
homework

C 🔊 Track 37 Listen. Say the numbers.

21 twenty-one	**22** twenty-two	**23** twenty-three	**24** twenty-four	**25** twenty-five
26 twenty-six	**27** twenty-seven	**28** twenty-eight	**29** twenty-nine	**30** thirty
31 thirty-one	**32** thirty-two	**33** thirty-three	**34** thirty-four	**35** thirty-five
36 thirty-six	**37** thirty-seven	**38** thirty-eight	**39** thirty-nine	**40** forty
50 fifty	**60** sixty	**70** seventy	**80** eighty	**90** ninety
100 one hundred				

D 🔊 **Track 38** Practice saying the numbers. Then listen and repeat.

22   36   45   59   64   71   88   97

E Read about Mimi. Complete the sentences with *am / is / are* or *have / has*.

    I (1)_____ British, but my aunt (2)_____ Australian. Her name (3)_____ Mimi. She (4)_____ long hair. She (5)_____ 48 years old. Mimi (6)_____ a husband. His name (7)_____ Marc. He (8)_____ short hair. He (9)_____ 52. Mimi and Marc (10) _____ good jobs. They (11)_____ doctors. Mimi and Marc (12)_____ in Sydney. They (13)_____ a nice home there. Sydney (14)_____ a beautiful city. It (15)_____ a famous bridge.

▶ **WORD BANK**
husband

NOTICE!▶
I am 17 years old.
(~~I have 17 years.~~)

F Read the sentences about a young woman, Lourdes Leon, and her famous mother. Complete them with *is / are* or *have / has*.

1. Lourdes ____is____ young.
2. She _____ a student.
3. She _____ a younger brother.
4. His name _____ Rocco Ritchie.
5. She and her mother _____ long hair.

6. They _____ good friends.
7. Her mother _____ a famous singer.
8. She _____ a lot of popular songs.
9. She _____ from the US.
10. She _____ around 60 years old.

G 🔁 Work with a partner. Check your answers in **F**. Then guess:

Lourdes has a famous mother. Her name is _____.

H Think of a person from a famous family.
Write sentences about the person in the chart.

Name of person:	
From	
Age	
Appearance	
Job	
Family	

I 🔁 Tell a partner about your person. Don't say the name!
Your partner guesses.

> He's British. He's from London. He's around 35, and he has an older brother. He has red hair. His mother is famous.

3 SPEAKING

A Say the sentences in the Useful Language box with your teacher.

B 🔊 Track 39 Read and listen to the conversation.

MARIE: That's a great photo of you.
COLIN: Thanks.
MARIE: And who's that? Your brother?
COLIN: No. That's my cousin.
MARIE: You look like him!
COLIN: Yeah, but he's younger.
MARIE: Oh? How old is he?
COLIN: He's nineteen.

C 🗨 Work with a partner. Say the conversation in **B**.

Useful Language
Describe appearance
You look like your brother / sister. You look like him / her.
Ask about age
How old are you? / How old is he?
I'm 21.   He's 19.

D 🔊 **Track 40** Listen. Write the words and numbers.

1. **A:** That's a great photo of you.

   B: Thanks.

   A: And who's that? Your _____?

   B: No. That's my _____.
   She's only _____.

   A: You look like _____!

   B: Yeah, I know.

2. **A:** That's a great photo of you.

   B: Thanks.

   A: And who's that? Your _____?

   B: No. That's my _____.

   A: Really? How old is _____?

   B: _____!

E 🤝 Work with a partner. Say the conversations in **D**.

F Find a family photo on your phone. Complete the sentences.

Example: ___This is my brother and his wife. They're on vacation in Paris.___

▶ **WORD BANK**
on vacation
wife

1. This is _____

2. He's / She's…   We're…   They're…

   ☐ at home   ☐ on vacation

   ☐ at school   ☐ _____

G 👥 Work in a small group.

1. Show your photo. Say your sentences from **F**.

2. Each person says a sentence or asks a question.

   A: This is my brother and his wife. They're on vacation in Paris.

   B: That's a great photo!

   A: Thanks.

   C: You look like your brother, but he has short hair. You have long hair.

   A: Yeah, I know!

   B: How old is your brother?

   A: He's 30.

H 👥 Repeat **G** with a new group.

8 MY FAVORITES

1 VOCABULARY

A 🔊 Track 41 Listen and repeat.

Movies and TV shows	funny 😄 popular 👏 sad 😞 scary 😮
Music	dance 🕺 hip hop 🧢 pop 🎤 rock 🎸

B Look at the photos on page 52. Complete the sentences (1–8) with a word.

▶ **WORD BANK**
band / group
singer
song

1. She's a Korean ___pop___ singer.

2. They're in a _____ band.

3. He's a _____ singer.

4. She listens to _____ music.

5. It's a _____ TV show.

6. It's a _____ video.

7. It's a _____ movie.

8. *Game of Thrones* is a _____ TV show around the world.

C 🔊 Track 42 Listen and check your answers in **B**.

D Write the words.

1. ads   _____sad_____

2. phi oph   _____

3. acsry   _____

4. opp   _____

5. nufyn   _____

6. upporal   _____

7. korc   _____

8. acden   _____

E Write ideas in your notebook.

Name a _____ movie or TV show.

1. funny

2. popular

3. sad

4. scary

Name a famous _____.

5. dance music DJ

6. hip hop singer

7. pop song

8. rock group

F 🔁 Work with a partner. Say your ideas in **E**. Are any of your answers the same?

Game of Thrones is a popular TV show.

Shakira is a famous hip hop artist.

2 GRAMMAR

A Study the charts.

Affirmative Statements			
I / You	like		
He / She	like**s**	hip hop.	**Notice!** Add *–s* or (*–es*) to the verb after *he / she / it*.
We / They	like		

Negative Statements				
I / You	don't			
He / She	doesn't	like	hip hop.	*don't = do not*
We / They	don't			*doesn't = does not*

B 🔊 Track 43 Look at the pictures. Listen and repeat.

PLAY VIDEO GAMES

WATCH MOVIES

THE DETECTIVE

READ COMIC BOOKS

POWER-MAN

NOTICE!▶
watch movies
~~look at movies~~

C Circle the correct words.

1. I (have / has) a brother. We are very different.

2. I (like / likes) dance music. He (don't / doesn't) like it.

3. He (play / plays) video games. I (play / plays) soccer.

4. I (don't / doesn't) watch scary movies. He (watch / watches) them a lot.

5. He (read / reads) magazines. I (read / reads) comic books.

6. There is one thing we both do. We both (study / studies) English!

NOTICE!▶
watch ⟶ watch**es**
study ⟶ stud**ies**

D 🔊 **Track 44** **PRONUNCIATION** Read the sentences. Then listen and repeat.

1. She <u>plays</u> video games.

2. He <u>watches</u> funny movies.

3. Ms. Davis <u>reads</u> long books.

4. Our teacher <u>writes</u> a lot.

E Write true sentences about a friend or a family member. Use the sentences in **C** as a model.

I have a friend. Her name is Maria. We are very different.

She studies hard. I don't study a lot.

_____

_____

_____

_____

F Complete the chart. Write sentences about yourself.

	True Statements	False Statements
	I don't like sad movies.	I like sad movies.
1		
2		
3		
4		

G  Work with a partner. Read a sentence. Your partner guesses true or false. Take turns.

I like sad movies.

True?

I'm sorry. It's false.

H 🔄 Work with a new partner. Play the game again.

My Favorites **55**

3 SPEAKING

A Say the sentences in the Useful Language box with your teacher.

B 🔊 Track 45 Read and listen to the conversation.

MATT: What's on TV?

KEN: Well, there's a soccer game.

MATT: What else?

KEN: *The Walking Dead* is on. Do you like that show?

MATT: No, not really. It's scary. Do you like it?

KEN: Yeah, I love it! It's my favorite show.

C Complete the sentences with a partner.

1. Matt / Ken likes *The Walking Dead.*
   It's a funny / his favorite show.

2. Matt / Ken doesn't like the show.
   He says, "It's boring / scary."

3. I like / don't like movies and TV shows with zombies.

D Say the conversation in **B**.

> **Useful Language**
>
> **Talk about likes and dislikes**
>
> Do you like…?
>   Yes! I love it! 🙂
>   Yeah, it's OK. 😐
>   No, not really. 🙁

The Walking Dead **is a TV show about zombies.**

E Say the conversation again. This time, talk about a TV show you know. Use the Useful Language box to help you.

Do you like the show *Game of Thrones*?

It's OK. Do you like it?

F Look again at **E** on page 53. Write each of your ideas on a small piece of paper.

Scary TV Show:
The Walking Dead

Pop song:
Hello (by Adele)

G Work in a small group. Take turns.

1. Put all the papers from **F** together on a desk.

2. One person takes a paper.

3. He or she asks the group a *Do you like…?* question.

4. The other students answer and explain.

Pop song:
Hello (by Adele)

Do you like the pop song "Hello" by Adele?

Yeah, I love it. Her music is great.

Not really. I like Adele, but I don't like that song.

I don't know that song.

NOTICE! ▶
Do you like the song "Hello"?
  Yeah, I love <u>it</u>.
Do you like Adele?
  Yeah, I love <u>her</u>.

9 TIME

1 VOCABULARY

A 🔊 **Track 46** Listen and repeat.

1. It's three (o'clock).

2. It's three-oh-five.
five after three.

3. It's three ten.
ten after three.

4. It's three fifteen.

5. It's three thirty.

6. It's three forty-five.
a quarter to four.

7. It's three fifty.
ten to four.

8. It's three fifty-five.
five to four.

B Work with a partner. Cover the sentences in **A**.
STUDENT A: Point to a clock. Ask the question.
STUDENT B: Say the time.

C Change roles. Repeat **B**.

D Draw four different times in your notebook.

What time is it?

It's…

It's noon.

It's midnight.

E Show your clocks to a partner. Ask for the time.

F Track 47 Listen and repeat.

Maya's schedule today			
Start time	**Classes**	**Start time**	**Classes**
	English		history
	science		break
	math		art
	lunch		P.E.

▶ **WORD BANK**
start

G Track 48 Listen to Maya's schedule. Write the times in the chart.

H Work with a partner. Ask and answer questions about Maya's schedule.

What time is her English class?

It's at nine.

What time is her break?

NOTICE!▶
What time is it (now)?
  It's 2:15.
What time is your class?
  It's <u>at</u> 2:30.

I Make your class schedule for today. Use the words in **F**.

J Work with a partner. Tell him / her about your schedule.

My English class is at…

2 GRAMMAR

A  Track 49 Look at the pictures. Listen and say the words.

MORNING
AFTERNOON
EVENING

Before **After**

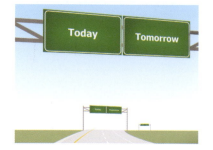

B Study the chart.

Questions with *when* and Time Expressions			
When is English class?	It's	at	2:00.
		in	the morning / afternoon / evening.
		before / after	math.
		now / later.	
		today / tomorrow.	

C Study the schedule. Complete the sentences. Use the words in the box.

Afternoon Schedule	
Start time	**Classes and Activities**
2:15	art
3:10	P.E.
4:30	study group (test tomorrow)

▶ **WORD BANK**
test

after	at	before	in	now	tomorrow

1. Art class is ___now___.

2. Art class is _____ P.E.

3. My study group is _____ P.E.

4. The big test is _____.

5. P.E. is _____ 3:10.

6. Art class is _____ the afternoon.

D Check your answers with a partner. Ask questions.

When is art class? It's now.

E Read the conversation. Find five more errors. Correct them.

A: What time is our lunch break?

B: It's in 12:00.

A: Then when science class is?

B: It's at 1:00.

A: Oh, so it's at the afternoon.

B: Yes, before lunch.

A: Got it. What time our test?

B: The test isn't today. It's ~~now~~. tomorrow

F 🔊 Track 50 Listen to the conversations. Match each one to a picture.

► **WORD BANK**
reservation

Conversation 1 ____   Conversation 2 ____   Conversation 3 ____

G 🔊 🔁 Track 51 Read the conversations. Listen again. Write the missing words. Then practice the conversations with a partner.

CONVERSATION 1

A: _____ is your reservation?

B: _____.

A: Are you all here _____?

B: Yes, we are.

A: Please come with me.

CONVERSATION 2

A: _____ is your test?

B: It's _____.

A: _____ is it tomorrow?

B: It's at _____ in the _____.

A: Good luck!

CONVERSATION 3

A: _____ is swim practice?

B: It's _____ school.

A: Is it _____?

B: No, it's tomorrow at _____.

A: Thanks.

H Use the words in the box. Complete the sentences to make them true for you.

| before school | in the morning |
| after school | in the afternoon |

► **WORD BANK**
School clubs and activities:
computer club, drama club,
English club
swim practice, band practice

1. My favorite class is _____.

2. My favorite part of the school day is _____.

3. My favorite club is _____.

4. My favorite activity is _____.

I 🔁 Ask a partner questions. Guess the answers.

When is your favorite part of the school day?

It's in the afternoon.

Is it lunchtime?

Yes!

3 SPEAKING

A Say the sentences in the Useful Language box with your teacher.

B 🔊 **Track 52** Read and listen to the conversation.

> A: Our big test is tomorrow.
>
> B: Yeah, I know. Let's study together.
>
> A: That sounds good. When?
>
> B: At 2:00?
>
> A: Sorry, I can't. I have class. Are you free later… at 3:30?
>
> B: Yeah. Let's meet then.

C 🔗 Answer the questions with a partner.

1. The students in **B** have a test. When is it?

2. They plan to study together. When?

D 🔗 Work with a partner. Say the conversation in **B**.

NOTICE! ▶
have + activity:
have class
    swim practice
    a test
    an appointment

E Cover the Useful Language box and the conversation in **B**.
Read the conversations below. Guess the missing words.

▶ **WORD BANK**
go shopping, shoes

1. A: Let's see the new Batman movie _____.

   B: I _____. I _____ a lot of homework.

   A: Are you _____ tomorrow?

   B: Yeah, _____ the afternoon.

   A: Great. There's a movie at _____.

   B: OK, _____ see it then.

   A: That sounds _____!

2. A: I need new shoes.

   B: Me too. Let's go shopping _____ school.

   A: Sorry, I _____. I _____ soccer practice.

   B: Are you free _____?

   A: Yeah, at _____.

   B: _____ go shopping then.

   A: Sounds _____!

F 🔊 Track 53 Listen. Write the words and the times in the conversations in **E**.

G 🗣 Work with a partner. Say the conversations in **E**.

H Write your schedule for today and tomorrow. List 4–5 activities each day.

	Today	Tomorrow
9:00 AM		
10:00		
11:00		
Noon		
1:00 PM		
2:00		
3:00		
4:00		
5:00		
6:00		
7:00		
8:00		

I 🗣 Find a time to do the activities with a partner.

- study for a test
- see a movie
- go shopping

> Let's study for our history test.

> Sounds good. When?

> Are you free today at...?

> No, sorry. I have class. Are you free at...?

1 GRAMMAR

A Study the chart.

Statements			Yes / No Questions			
You	like		Do	you		
She	likes	hip hop.	Does	she	like	hip hop?
They	like		Do	they		
In questions, *do / does* comes first.						

B Write questions.

1. You have a big family. ⟶ <u>Do you have a big family?</u>

2. She likes her aunt. _____

3. The cafe closes soon. _____

4. He has class now. _____

5. They like English class. ⟶ _____

6. We have swim practice now. _____

C Write statements and questions. Follow the pattern.

▶ **WORD BANK**
pet

A	B	C	D	E
do	he	don't	has	a pet
does	you	doesn't	have	

NOTICE!▶
Affirmative and negative
I like… / She likes…
I don't like… / She doesn't like…

1. (**B, D, E**) <u>He has a pet.</u>

2. (**B, D, E**) _____

3. (**B, C, D, E**) <u>He</u> _____

4. (**B, C, D, E**) _____

5. (**A, B, D, E**) <u>Do</u> _____

6. (**A, B, D, E**) _____

D Write affirmative statements (+), negative statements (–), and questions (?). Use the words.

English / they / study

(+) 1. <u>They study English.</u>

(–) 2. _____

(?) 3. _____

questions / ask / the teacher

(+) 4. <u>The teacher asks questions.</u>

(–) 5. _____

(?) 6. _____

Paula / music / listen to

(+) 7. _____

(–) 8. _____

(?) 9. _____

I / the answer / know

(+) 10. _____

(–) 11. _____

(?) 12. _____

E Study the chart.

Yes / No Questions				Short Answers	
Do	you	like	math?	Yes, I do.	No, I don't.
Does	he she	read	comic books?	Yes, he does. Yes, she does.	No, he doesn't. No, she doesn't.
Do	we they	have	homework?	Yes, we do. Yes, they do.	No, we don't. No, they don't.

F 🔊 Track 54 Circle the correct questions and short answers. Then listen and check your answers.

1a. Do I know you?

    Does I know you?

1b. Yes, I do.

    Yes, you do.

2a. Do they play video games?

    Does they play video games?

2b. Yes, do they.

    Yes, they do.

3a. Do the store open at 10:00?

    Does the store open at 10:00?

3b. Yes, it doesn't.

    No, it doesn't.

G Put the words in order. Write questions.

1. a lot of / you / homework / have / do _____

2. best friend / to / go / your / does / your / school _____

3. does / answer / your / your / teacher / questions _____

4. you / do / have / family / big / a _____

5. classmates / class / English / your / do / like _____

H 🔁 Work with a partner. Ask and answer the questions in **G**.

Do you have a lot of homework?

Yes, I do. I'm busy!

1. _____ 2. _____

3. _____ 4. _____

5. *Luke* _____ 6. *Best Friend* _____

2 SEE IT AND SAY IT

A   Find Luke. Point to each person in his family and tell a partner. Write your answers.

B   **Track 55** Read the conversations. Guess the answers. Then listen and check your answers. Match the people to the conversations.

She's his sister.

CONVERSATION A _____

A: What _____ is it?

B: It's 8:00.

A: Oh, good. *The Voice* is _____.

B: I don't know it.

A: It's a show with _____. Watch.

B: Wow! He's really good!

A: Yeah, and he's only _____.

CONVERSATION B _____

A: Do you _____ video games?

B: Yes, I do. This one is my favorite.

It's _____.

A: Is it difficult?

B: No, not really.

_____ play it!

CONVERSATION C _____

A: What time is *Family Guy* _____?

B: At 8:30.

A: Oh no. It's only 8 PM. No problem. Let's watch it now.

B: I _____ like *Family Guy*. It's boring.

A: I love it! It's _____!

C   Work with a partner. Choose one conversation. Change the blue words. Make your own conversation.

3 ARE YOU FREE AT 2:00?

A  Work with a partner.

STUDENT A: Look at this page.   **STUDENT B:** Turn to page 105.

Student A

Read your schedule silently. What activities are there? When are they?

▶ **WORD BANK**
homeroom

	Today	Tomorrow
8:00 AM		Study group
8:45	Homeroom	Homeroom
9:00	English	TOEFL class
10:10	Science	Science
11:15	Drama club	
12:00 PM	Lunch	Lunch
1:00	Math	Math
2:00		
3:10		Art history
4:10		
5:00	Soccer practice	
5:30		Doctor's appointment
6:00		

B You want to add the two activities below to your schedule. When are you free? Think of times.

work on your science project   play Pokemon Go

C  Ask your partner to do the two activities in **B**. Find a good time for both of you. Then write the activities on the schedule above.

NOTICE!▶
You can say:
I'm free at 8:00 AM.
          before school.
          in the morning.

> Let's work on our science project today.

> Sounds good. When?

> Are you free at...?

> No. I have... I'm free...

D  Your partner wants to ask you to do two activities. Listen and look at your schedule. Find a good time for both of you. Write each activity on your schedule.

1 VOCABULARY

A 🔊 **Track 56** Listen and repeat.

get up

take a shower

get dressed

go to school

start (school)

finish (school)

go home

do homework

go to bed

Every day, millions of people go to school or work by subway.

B Cover **A**. Complete the sentences. Use the words in the box.

do	finish	get	go	start	take

My daily routine

▶ **WORD BANK**
routine

1. I _____ up at 6:30.

2. Then I _____ a shower, and I _____ dressed.

3. At 7:30, I _____ to school. Classes _____ at 8:30.

4. After school, I have swim practice at 3:30. I _____ practice at 5:00.

5. Then I _____ home and _____ homework.

6. In the evening, I watch TV or play video games. Then I _____ to bed at 11:00.

C 🔁 Say the sentences in **B** with a partner.

D 👥 Work in a small group. Play the game.

1. Write each action in **A** on a small paper.

2. Mix the papers.

3. Take a paper. (Don't show your partners!)
   Do the action.

4. Your partners guess. The first correct answer gets
   a point.

5. Repeat steps 3 and 4 with all the words.

Take a shower!

E Write sentences about your daily routine. Use the words from **A**.

In the morning, I _____

In the afternoon, I _____

In the evening, I _____

F 🔁 Tell a partner about your day. Use your sentences in **E**.

G 🔁 Tell a new partner about your day.
This time, don't read your sentences.

In the morning, I get up at 7:00 AM. Then I...

2 GRAMMAR

A Look at the words. Say them with your teacher.

	Day 1	Day 2	Day 3	Day 4	Day 5	Day 6	Day 7	Day 8	Day 9	Day 10
always	✓	✓	✓	✓	✓	✓	✓	✓	✓	✓
usually	✓	✓	✓	✓	✓	✓	✓	✓	✓	
often	✓		✓	✓	✓		✓		✓	✓
sometimes	✓		✓		✓		✓		✓	
never										

B 🔁 Complete the sentence. Use a word from **A**. Tell a partner.

I _____ get up at around seven in the morning.

C Study the chart.

<table>
<tr><td colspan="5" align="center">Adverbs of Frequency</td></tr>
<tr><td>He</td><td><u>is</u></td><td>always / usually / often / sometimes / never</td><td>late.</td><td>The blue words come after be.</td></tr>
<tr><td>She</td><td>always / usually / often / sometimes / never</td><td>gets up</td><td>early.</td><td>The blue words come before other verbs.</td></tr>
</table>

► **WORD BANK**
early
late

D Read the sentences. Write new sentences. Use the blue words.

1. I do homework after school. (always)

   I always do homework after school.

2. I'm happy. (usually)

   _____

3. I watch movies in the evening. (sometimes)

   _____

4. I'm early to school. (often)

   _____

5. I miss class. (never)

   _____

6. I raise my hand in class. (often)

   _____

► **WORD BANK**
miss (class)

E 🔁 Say the sentences in **D**. Are the sentences true for you? Tell your partner.

> I always do homework after school. That's true for me.

> Not me. I *sometimes* do homework after school.

F Put the words in order. Write the sentences.

1. reads / books / she / comic / never

   _____

2. math / always / is / interesting / class

   _____

3. appointment / have / after school / an / sometimes / I

   _____

4. teacher / my / sad / never / is

   _____

5. a / in / cafe / study / they / usually

   _____

6. are / difficult / English / often / tests

   _____

NOTICE!▶
These sentences are both OK:
<u>Sometimes</u> I take the bus.
I take the bus <u>sometimes</u>.

G 🔁 Complete the sentences. Practice them with a partner.

▶ WORD BANK
choose
nervous

My First Day of Class			
In the evening (the night before)...	1. I _____ choose my clothes.	2. I _____ check my backpack.	3. _____ I go to bed early.	4. I am _____ nervous.
In the morning (the first day of class)...	5. I get up late _____.	6. I _____ take a shower.	7. I _____ go to class early.	8. I am _____ excited.

H 🔊 **Track 57** Listen. Write the missing words in **G**.

I 🔁 Think about the first day of school for you. What do you do? Tell a partner. Use adverbs.

> I usually choose my clothes the night before.

> Me too!

MONDAY
TUESDAY
WEDNESDAY
THURSDAY
FRIDAY
SATURDAY
SUNDAY

3 SPEAKING

A Look at the photo. Say the days of the week with your teacher. Then answer the questions.

1. What day is today? What day is tomorrow?

2. What is your favorite day of the week?

3. In your country, when is the weekend? Say the day(s).

▶ **WORD BANK**
weekend

B Say the sentences in the Useful Language box with your teacher.

C 🔊 Track 58 Read and listen to the conversation.

BILL: I'm so happy it's Friday! I need a break.

NADIA: Yeah, me too. What do you usually do on the weekend, Bill?

BILL: Not much. I get up late. Sometimes, I see my friends. What about you?

NADIA: Oh, I'm really busy. I have a class on Saturday morning. Then I work on Saturday afternoon. On Sunday, I do homework.

BILL: Wow, you *are* busy!

Useful Language
Talk about your weekend
What do you usually do on the weekend?
Not much. I get up late and...
I'm really busy. I have class and...

NOTICE!▶
on + day of the week
I work <u>on</u> Saturday.
<u>On</u> Sunday, I do homework.

D 🔁 Answer the questions with a partner.

1. On the weekend, what does Bill do? What does Nadia do?

2. On the weekend, who is busy? Who has a lot of free time?

E 🔁 Say the conversation in **C** with your partner.

F What do you do on the weekend? Check (✓) the activities.

_____ get up late	_____ go shopping
_____ do homework	_____ go to school
_____ see friends	_____ go to the gym
_____ play video games	_____ go to a club
_____ watch TV / a movie	_____ my idea: _____

NOTICE! ▶
go + verb *-ing*
I <u>go shopping</u>.

go to + a place
I <u>go to the gym</u> / <u>a club</u>.

G 🔁 Work with a partner. Say the conversation in **C** again. Use your own information and the ideas in **F**.

H 👥 Ask three classmates about their weekends. Complete the chart.

Classmate's name	What does he / she do on the weekend?
1.	
2.	
3.	

> What do you usually do on the weekend?

> Not much. On Saturday morning, I usually get up late. Then I...

I 🔁 Tell a new partner your answers in **H**. Are the people busy on the weekend or not?

> On the weekend, Sofia is really busy. On Saturday, she...

J 🔁 What are popular weekend activities in your class? Tell your partner.

1 VOCABULARY

A 🔊 Track 59 Listen and say the months of the year.

January	May	September
February	June	October
March	July	November
April	August	December

B 🔁 Work with a partner. Say the months. Then change roles and repeat.

Student A: Close your book. Say the months.

Student B: Check Student A's answers.

C Choose a month. Complete the sentence.

This month starts with the letter _____.

D 🔁 Cover the months in **A**. Say your sentence in **C**. Your partner says the month.

> This month starts with the letter *O*.   It's...

Young people in Spain walk to a summer mask festival.

🔊 **Track 60** Listen and repeat.

1st	**first**	11th	**eleventh**	21st	**twenty-first**
2nd	**second**	12th	**twelfth**	22nd	**twenty-second**
3rd	**third**	13th	**thirteenth**	23rd	**twenty-third**
4th	**fourth**	14th	**fourteenth**	24th	**twenty-fourth**
5th	**fifth**	15th	**fifteenth**	25th	**twenty-fifth**
6th	**sixth**	16th	**sixteenth**	26th	**twenty-sixth**
7th	**seventh**	17th	**seventeenth**	27th	**twenty-seventh**
8th	**eighth**	18th	**eighteenth**	28th	**twenty-eighth**
9th	**ninth**	19th	**nineteenth**	29th	**twenty-ninth**
10th	**tenth**	20th	**twentieth**	30th	**thirtieth**

F 🔊 **Track 61** Listen. Write the dates.

NOTICE! ▶ Say: Today is July fourth.
Write: July 4 *or* 7/4

1. ___July 4___   5. _____   9. _____

2. _____   6. _____   10. _____

3. _____   7. _____   11. _____

4. _____   8. _____   12. _____

G 🔁 Say the dates in **F** with a partner. Take turns.

H Complete the sentence. Write the month and day.

My birthday is on _____ _____.
month   day

NOTICE! ▶
My birthday is <u>in</u> May.
My birthday is <u>on</u> May 12.
My birthday is on the 31st (thirty-first).

I Write four different months in the chart.

Month	Name	Birthday

J 🔷 Play the game with your class.

1. Ask classmates *Is your birthday in…?*

2. When a person says *yes*, write his or her name and birthday.

3. Try to complete your chart first.

Is your birthday in July?

No, sorry. It's not.

Yes, it is. It's on July 1st.

2 GRAMMAR

A Study the chart.

Wh- Questions and Answers						
Yes / No question		Do	you	live	in Santiago?	Yes, I do. / No, I don't.
Wh- question	Where	**do**	you	live?		(I live) in Santiago.
Yes / No question		Do	they	study	in April?	Yes, they do. / No, they don't.
Wh- question	What	**do**	they	study?		(They study) math and science.
Yes / No question		Does	she	go	to school by bus?	Yes, she does. / No, she doesn't.
Wh- question	How	**does**	she	go	to school?	(She goes to school) by bus.

In *Wh-* questions with other verbs, use *do / does* instead of *am / is / are.*

B Match the questions and answers.

1. Where do you live? _____
2. Who do you live with? _____
3. What does your mother do? _____
4. How do you go to school? _____
5. When does your school year start? _____
6. What do you always bring to class? _____
7. What does your teacher usually say? _____
8. What do you do on your birthday? __f__

a. By car.
b. "Do your homework!"
c. In the city.
d. In April.
e. She's a businesswoman.
f. ~~I open presents.~~
g. My parents.
h. A notebook and a pen.

NOTICE!▶
I go to school <u>by</u> bus.

NOTICE!▶
What do you do? = What's your jo

C 🔄 Work with a partner. Ask and answer the questions in **B**.

Who do you live with? — I live with my parents and my brother.

D 🔊 Track 62 Dai is checking in to his new class. Complete the questions. Then listen and check your answers.

▶ **WORD BANK**
check in

DAI: Good morning. I'm Dai. Dai Suzuki.

WOMAN: Good morning, Dai. Hmm…OK, I see your name. You're checked in.

DAI: Thanks. _____ does the class _____?

WOMAN: You're in Room 11.

DAI: OK. How _____ I _____ there?

WOMAN: Go straight down the hall and turn right. It's the second door on your left.

DAI: Great. _____ _____ the class start?

WOMAN: Let's see… in about ten minutes.

DAI: Oh, and _____ does it _____?

WOMAN: At 9:15.

DAI: Thanks a lot.

E 🗩 Say the conversation in **D** with a partner. Use your own names and your own answers.

> You're in Room B.

> OK, thanks. How do I get there?

> Go up to the second floor. It's the first door on your right.

F 🗩 Work with a partner. Look up these words in your dictionary.

▶ **WORD BANK**
buy   serve   wear   have a party

NOTICE!▶
New Year's Day = January 1
New Year's Eve = December 31

G Think about New Year's Eve. Complete the YES and NO questions. Write the missing words.

Do you have a party on New Year's Eve?

YES	NO
__What__ do you buy for the party?	_____ do you do?
_____ do you start the party?	_____ do you go?
_____ do you invite?	_____ do you wear?
_____ do you serve?	_____ do you say?

H Think about the first question in **G**. Choose the YES or NO box and answer the questions.

I 🗩 Ask a partner the questions in **G**. Take turns. Are your plans similar or different?

A: Do you have a party on New Year's Eve?

B: Yes, we do.

A: What do you buy for the party?

B: We buy a lot of noisemakers.
How about you? Do you have a party?

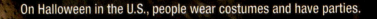

On Halloween in the U.S., people wear costumes and have parties.

3 SPEAKING

A Look at the picture. Answer the questions.

1. What do people do on Halloween?

2. Guess: When is Halloween? Say the date.

B Say the sentences in the Useful Language box with your teacher.

Useful Language	
Say you know or don't know something	
When is the Halloween party?	
certain	not certain
It's this Saturday.	I'm not sure. Is it on Saturday? I don't know. / I have no idea.

C ◁)) Track 63 Look at the calendar. Then read and listen to the conversation.

ZAC: When is the school Halloween party—Friday or Saturday?

CARLOS: I'm not sure. Check online.

ZAC: OK. Um, it's on Saturday, the thirtieth.

CARLOS: What time does it start?

ZAC: At 9:00. Let's go.

CARLOS: Sounds good!

Wed	Thurs	Fri	Sat
27 School food festival Noon	28	29 School film festival 6:30 PM	30 Halloween party 9:00 PM

D 🔁 Answer the questions with a partner.

1. When is the Halloween party? 2. What time does it start?

E 🔁 Work with a partner. Say the conversation in **C**.

F 🔁 Work with a partner. Say the conversation in **C** again.
Talk about the film festival. Use the information on the calendar
and a different expression.

▶ **WORD BANK**
film festival
food festival

G 🔁 Change roles. This time, talk about the food festival.

H Look at each important day. When is it? Write the date or check (✓) "Don't know."

Important days	Date	Don't know
the last day of school		☐
Mother's Day		☐
Earth Day		☐
the first day of winter		☐

▶ **WORD BANK**
last
spring, summer,
fall, winter

I 🔁 Work with a partner. Ask questions about the important days. Take turns.

When is Earth Day?

I'm not sure. Is it in the spring?

I have no idea. Do you know?

Yes, maybe. Check online.

J On your own, write four important days and their dates in your notebook.

K 🔁 Work with a partner. Play the game. Take turns.
Student A: Ask a *When is…?* question about a day in **J**.
Student B: Guess the correct answer and get points.

A: When is Father's Day?

B: I'm not sure. Is it in June?

A: Yes!

B: Is it June fifteenth?

A: No, sorry. It's June…

One point: For the correct month
Two points: For the correct month and day

12 FOOD

1 VOCABULARY

steak and fries

tea

cereal and fruit, coffee, orange juice

soup and salad with bread

pizza

chicken and rice

ice cream

pasta

A 🔊 Track 64 Look at the pictures. Listen and repeat.

Food vendors sell food in Central Market in Kota Bharu, Kelantan, Malaysia.

B 🔊 Track 65 Listen and repeat again. Notice *and*.

1. steak and fries
2. cereal and fruit

3. soup and salad
4. chicken and rice

NOTICE!▶
steak <u>and</u> fries =
steak <u>n</u> fries

C 🔄 Work with a partner. Cover the words under the photos. Say the food and drinks.

D 🔊 Track 66 Say the words in the Word Bank.
Then listen to the speaker. Number the photos (1–8) on page 80.

E 🔊 Track 67 Read the sentences. Guess the answers.
Then listen again. Write the word.

▶ WORD BANK
breakfast, lunch, dinner
dessert

eat (lunch)
drink (coffee)

Say you like a food
This soup is <u>delicious / good</u>.

The girl says…

1. First, I need my _____.

2. This is my favorite dinner: _____!

3. It's _____ again for lunch… my _____ time this week!

4. The Moroccan mint _____ here is delicious!

5. Dinner tonight is _____ and _____ from the restaurant near school.

6. This _____ is really good.

7. The _____ at this restaurant is delicious. The _____ are good, too.

8. Lunch today is my mom's homemade _____ and a _____.

F 🔄 What food and drinks on page 80 do you like? Circle them. Then ask a partner.

> Do you like steak?

> No. I don't eat meat. Do you like steak?

> Yeah, I love it!

G 🔄 Complete the sentences. Then say your sentences to a partner.
Your partner asks a question.

I usually eat _____ for breakfast / lunch / dinner.

I always / sometimes / never eat dessert after dinner.

I eat / drink a lot of _____.

▶ WORD BANK
milk
soda
water

> I always eat dessert after dinner.

> Really? What do you eat?

> Fruit.

2 GRAMMAR

A 🔊 Track 68 Look at the pictures. Listen and repeat.

a **bowl** of rice   a **cup** of coffee   a **slice** of bread

a **glass** of water   a **piece** of cake   a **bag** of chips

B Study the chart.

Quantity Expressions			
I want	some	rice.	I want a bowl of rice.
		coffee.	I want a cup of coffee.
		bread.	I want a slice of bread.
		water.	I want a glass of water.
		cake.	I want a piece of cake.
		chips.	I want a bag of chips.

Use *some* to talk about a general amount. Use *a + bowl / cup / slice / glass / piece / bag + of* to talk about part of a whole amount.

C Write the missing words.

1. ___a bowl of___ pasta
2. _____ popcorn
3. _____ pie
4. _____ cereal
5. _____ tea
6. _____ pizza
7. _____ milk
8. _____ soup

popcorn

pie

D ⟳ Compare your answers in **C** with a partner's answers.

E Will is home from school. Read the conversation. Guess the missing words.   ▶ **WORD BANK**
        snack, hungry, healthy

WILL: Mom, can I have a snack?

MOM: Will, it's 4:30 now. Dinner is in an hour.

WILL: But, Mom, I'm hungry!

MOM: OK. Do you want a piece
      of _____?
      We have some oranges.

WILL: No, I want some _____.

MOM: No, Will, that's for dessert.

WILL: OK, can I have some _____?

MOM: No, that's not healthy. Eat a small bowl
      of _____, or drink a glass of
      _____.

WILL: OK.

F 🔊 Track 69 Listen to the conversation in **E**. Check your answers.

G ⟳ Write your own conversation.
Use **E** as a model. Say it with a partner.

> I'm hungry!   Do you want a piece of cherry pie?

> I don't like cherry pie. Can I have a slice of pizza?

H ⚙ Read the instructions. Work in a group. Play the game.

1. Write the words in ❶ on pieces of paper two times.

2. Write the words in ❷ on pieces of paper one time.

3. Mix the papers together. Put them face down on the desk.

4. Take turns. Turn over two papers. Make a match!

❶	
a bag of	a glass of
a bowl of	a piece of
a cup of	a slice of

❷			
bread	coffee	orange juice	popcorn
cereal	fruit	pie	rice
chips	milk	pizza	tea

A food truck sells food at lunchtime in Calgary, Alberta in Canada.

3 SPEAKING

A [icon] Look at the photo. Answer the questions with a partner.

1. Are there food trucks in your city?

2. Do you buy food on the street?

B Say the sentences in the Useful Language box with your teacher.

C [icon] Track 70 Read and listen to the conversation.

SERVER: Who's next?

PAULA: Hi, I'd like the chicken sandwich, please.

SERVER: Anything else?

PAULA: Yeah, a bottle of water and a bag of chips.

SERVER: OK. The chicken sandwich, a bottle of water, and a bag of chips. That's $6.50.

PAULA: Here you go.

SERVER: Thanks. And here's your food.

D [icon] Work with a partner. Say the conversation in **C**.

Useful Language
Order food and drinks
I'd like the chicken sandwich, (please). Anything else? A bag of chips, (please). / No, thanks.
Paying
That's $6.50. (*six fifty*) Here you go.

E 🗘 Work with a partner.

Say the conversation in **C** again.

Order from the menu.

NOTICE!▶

We say: *a bottle of water*

But for other drinks we say:

a soda, an orange juice, an iced tea

THE CHICKEN FEED

— MENU —

CHICKEN AND RICE PLATE $4.50

CHICKEN SANDWICH $3.50

CHICKEN SALAD $3.75

CHICKEN TACO $2.25

— EXTRAS —

A BAG OF CHIPS $1.00

A BOWL OF CHICKEN SOUP $2.50

— DRINKS —

WATER $2.00

ORANGE JUICE $2.50

SODA $1.75

ICED TEA $1.25

F 🗘 Change roles. Repeat **E**.

G 🗘 Work with a partner. Make your own food truck.

1. Choose a type of food or drink for the truck, or write your own idea.

   coffee and tea   Italian food   sandwiches   our idea: _____

2. Give your food truck a name. Write a menu with five or six items. Put the menu on the wall.

H 👥 Get into two groups (A and B).

Student A: You are the server. Stay at your desk with your menu. Ask for people's orders.

Student B: You're hungry. Go to three food trucks and order something. Write your orders below.

Food Truck Name	My Order
Example: *Dessert Heaven*	*chocolate cake*
1.	1.
2.	2.
3.	3.

Who's next?

Hi, I'd like the chocolate cake, please.

I 👥 Change roles. Repeat **H**.

J 🗘 Talk about your orders with a partner. Use the sentence.

At (name of food truck),

I ordered _____.

At Yasmin's Food Truck, I ordered a cup of mint tea and...

1 GRAMMAR

A Read the questions. Match a picture with a question.

_____ 1. Who do you live with?

_____ 2. What do you do on the weekend?

_____ 3. When is your birthday?

_____ 4. Where is your hometown?

B Complete the questions. Write the missing question words.

Who	What	When	Where

1. _____ do you watch on TV?

2. _____ is summer vacation?

3. _____ do you buy food in your neighborhood?

4. _____ does your father do?

5. _____ do you live with?

6. _____ do you go to school?

7. _____ is your nickname?

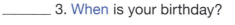

What do you watch on TV?

The Voice. It's my favorite show.

C 🔁 Work with a partner. Ask and answer the questions in **B**.

D Study the charts.

Yes / No and *Wh-* Questions with *be*				
Statement		I	am	Peruvian.	
***Yes / No* Question**		Are	you	Peruvian?	Yes, I am. / No, I'm not.
***Wh-* Question**	Where	are	you	from?	(I'm from) Peru.

Yes / No and *Wh-* Questions with Other Verbs						
Statement			I	live	in	Japan.	
***Yes / No* Question**		Do	you	live	in	Tokyo?	Yes, I do. / No, I don't.
***Wh-* Question**	Where	do	you	live	exactly?		(I live in) Nezu.

E Write questions. Follow the pattern.

► **WORD BANK**
dish

A	B	C	D	E	F	G	H
What	dish dishes	do is	your you	like	favorite pasta	food	pasta

1. (**A, B, C, D, E**) _____

2. (**A, C, D, F, G**) _____

3. (**C, D, E, F**) _____

4. (**C, D, F, G, H**) _____

F 🔁 Ask your partner the questions in **E**. Write his or her answers in your notebook.

G Write the questions. Put the words in order.

1. free / after / you / school / are

   _____

2. do / what / have / you / breakfast / for

   _____

3. your / is / name / what / teacher's

   _____

4. you / go / bed / do / early / to

   _____

5. is / class / fun / your / English

   _____

6. start / school / when / does

   _____

7. over / 50 / are / parents / your

   _____

8. for / family / does / go out / your / dinner

   _____

9. where / your / is / school

   _____

10. sing / does / singer / your / in English / favorite

    _____

H Match the questions in **G** to their answers below.

_____ a. No, they're not.

_____ b. Juice and cereal.

_____ c. Yes, she does.

_____ d. It's on Bank Street.

_____ e. Yes, it is.

_____ f. At 7:50 in the morning.

_____ g. Yes, they do.

_____ h. No, I'm not.

_____ i. Yes, I do.

_____ j. Mr. Ruiz.

I 🔁 Work with a partner. Write a conversation. Use a question from **G** in your conversation.

J 🔵 Find another pair. Say your conversation.

A: Does your family go out for dinner?

B: Not usually. Does your family go out for dinner?

A: Yes. Sometimes we go to a Chinese restaurant on the weekend.

B: What restaurant do you go to?

2 SEE IT AND SAY IT

A Look at the picture. What food and drinks do you see? Write the quantities and the words.

<u>   a bowl of ice cream   </u>   _____   _____

_____   _____   _____

B Read the sentences about the picture in **A**. Circle *True* or *False*. Rewrite the false sentences to make them true.

1. It's a New Year's party.	True	(False)	<u> It's a birthday party. </u>
2. The party is for Catalina.	True	False	_____
3. It's summer.	True	False	_____
4. The party is in the evening.	True	False	_____
5. The party is in October.	True	False	_____
6. The party is at seven o'clock.	True	False	_____

3 WHAT DO YOU USUALLY DO ON YOUR BIRTHDAY?

A Read the conversations. Guess the answers.

CONVERSATION 1

A: What do you usually do on your birthday?

B: I usually have a _____ party. But not this year.

A: Why is that?

B: My birthday is on _____ this year. It's not a _____ day for a party.

CONVERSATION 2

A: What do you usually do on your birthday?

B: I eat _____ with my family at _____.

A: What do you eat?

B: My mom makes steaks, and we have _____ for dessert!

B 🔊 Track 71 Listen. Complete the conversations in **A**.

C 🗣 Ask a partner: What do you usually do on your birthday?

4 THE QUESTION GAME

A Read the questions below. If your answer is *yes*, put a check (✓) in the *Me* column.

Do you...	Me	Classmate's Name	*Wh-* Question	Answer
1. get up late on the weekend?			When...?	
2. always eat breakfast?			What...?	
3. do homework after school?			Where...?	
4. see friends on the weekend?			Who...?	
5. have an older sister?			What...?	
6. live near school?			Where...?	
7. like hip hop music?			Who...?	
8. have a birthday in the spring?			When...?	

B 👥 Talk to different classmates. Complete the chart in **A**.

1. For each question, find a different person to say *yes*.

2. Write the classmate's name.

3. Ask a *Wh-* question to get more information.

4. Write the person's answer.

5. Complete your chart first and win.

6. Tell the class your answers.

> Do you get up late on the weekend?

> When do you usually get up?

> Yes, I do.

> At noon.

A Unscramble the letters. Write the word.

1. nletis __listen__

2. rlciec _____

3. taerep _____

4. croev _____

5. sernwa _____

6. seclo _____

B Circle the correct word.

1. (**Write** / Listen) your name.

2. (Circle / Close) your book.

3. (Cover / Say) the page.

4. (Open / Answer) the question.

5. (Ask / Raise) your hand.

6. (Look / Read) at the picture.

C Match the statements.

__c__ 1. Good evening.

____ 2. Say the number.

____ 3. Listen and repeat. C-o-v-e-r.

____ 4. Open your book to page 4.

____ 5. Write your name.

____ 6. Good afternoon.

a. Can you repeat that, please?

b. Five.

c. ~~Good evening.~~

d. C-o-v-e-r.

e. Emily.

f. Good afternoon.

D Write the words and expressions in the correct place in the chart.

Read the conversation.	Say the word.
Good afternoon.	two
~~three~~	Good evening.
Write your name.	Can you say that again, please?
Circle the answer.	five

Numbers	Greetings	Instructions	Asking to repeat
three			

E Write the sentences. Use the words.

1. you / that / can / repeat / ? __Can you repeat that?__

2. into / get / groups / small / . _____

3. 5 / look / page / at / . _____

4. the / sentence / read / . _____

5. say / you / that / can / again / ? _____

6. your / write / name / . _____

2 MY NAME IS...

A Write your name. Write the names of four classmates.

My name is . . .	Classmates
Diego Rodriguez	1. 2. 3. 4.

B Complete the sentences with the correct word.

He	I	She	You

1. _____I_____ am a student.

2. _____ is a teacher. (Mrs. Jones)

3. _____ are a doctor.

4. _____ is a teacher. (Mr. Baker)

5. _____ is a businesswoman.

C Rewrite the underlined contraction in each sentence.

1. <u>I'm</u> a programmer.   _____I am_____

2. <u>You're</u> a teacher.   _____

3. <u>He's</u> a businessman.   _____

4. <u>She's</u> a soccer player.   _____

5. <u>I'm</u> a businesswoman.   _____

D Write the words and phrases in the correct place in the chart.

I'm John. Hello.	Hi. It's nice to meet you.	My name is Helen. ~~Nice to meet you, too.~~

Greet someone	Say your name	Meet someone
		Nice to meet you, too.

E Complete the conversation with the correct words.

he's	~~Hi~~	is	meet	Nice	too

TEACHER: _____Hi_____. I'm Mrs. Harris.

STUDENT: Hello. My name _____ Maya.

TEACHER: Nice to _____ you, Maya.

STUDENT: _____ to meet you, Mrs. Harris.

3 OUR CLASSROOM

A Write the words. Use the letters.

1. coaekbso   b*ookcase*_____
2. ctperoum   c_____
3. rsreae   e_____
4. blmeralu   u_____
5. iycriadnto   d_____
6. deworbitah   w_____

B Write the words for the numbers.

1. 1 _____*one*_____
2. 4 _____
3. 2 _____
4. 5 _____
5. 3 _____

C Complete the sentences. Use *a*, *an* or Ø.

1. It's ____*a*____ clock.
2. They're _____ backpacks.
3. It's _____ umbrella.
4. It's _____ screen.
5. They're _____ erasers.
6. It's _____ whiteboard.

D Write the contractions.

1. they are = _____*they're*_____
2. you are = _____
3. he is = _____
4. she is = _____
5. it is = _____
6. what is = _____

E Correct the sentences.

1. Can I use an pencil?   _____*Can I use a pencil?*_____
2. Youare welcome.   _____
3. What'is this?   _____
4. It's a umbrella.   _____
5. They're laptop.   _____
6. What is these?   _____

4 PERSONAL INFORMATION

A Write the number.

1. 10 _____ten_____
2. 11 _____
3. 12 _____
4. 8 _____
5. 15 _____

6. 12 _____
7. 20 _____
8. 9 _____
9. 18 _____
10. 19 _____

B Write the information.

| email address   phone number   student ID number   student name |

1. 97-56-93 _____student ID number_____
2. 555-2908 _____
3. Margarita Ortiz _____
4. AntonK@Ymail.com _____
5. 98-36-74 _____
6. MTran@university.edu _____

C Write the correct word.

1. (I) _____My_____ name is Octavio.
2. What's (it) _____ name?
3. Is this (you) _____ pencil?
4. He is (they) _____ teacher.
5. This is (we) _____ classroom.

6. (He) _____ email address is PabloB@linkmail.com.
7. (I) _____ phone number is (228) 555-2015.
8. This is (she) _____ student ID number.

D Match the questions with the answers.

__e__ 1. Is this his book?
_____ 2. What is their phone number?
_____ 3. What's your name?
_____ 4. Are they your friends?
_____ 5. Is our class in Room 18?
_____ 6. What's her email address?

a. 555-2987
b. MayaR@starlink.net
c. Yes, they are.
d. No, it's in 14.
e. ~~Yes, it is.~~
f. My name is Ahmed.

E Put the conversation in the correct order.

_____ Yeah. It's 555-1043. It's new.
__1__ Hello?
_____ Is this Akira?

_____ It's your classmate, Sheila.
_____ Oh, hi Sheila! Sorry! Your number is different.
_____ Yes, it's Akira. Uh, excuse me, who's calling?

5 MY NEIGHBORHOOD

A Match the words.

__e__ 1. cafe

_____ 2. ATM

_____ 3. car

_____ 4. neighborhood

_____ 5. store

_____ 6. subway station

a. bank

b. home

c. supermarket

d. bus stop

e. ~~coffee shop~~

f. garage

B Write your favorite place.

1. supermarket _My favorite supermarket is Family Foods._

2. movie theater _____

3. city _____

4. restaurant _____

5. clothing store _____

6. park _____

C Write the words in the correct place in the chart.

bank   cars   ~~garage~~   movie theater   park   supermarkets

There is a . . .	There are some / no / two . . .
garage	

D Write sentences. Use *There is / There's* or *There are*.

1. a park in my neighborhood _____ _There's a park in my neighborhood._ _____

2. some trees in the park _____

3. no ATMs on my street _____

4. a post office near here _____

5. two coffee shops on Main Street _____

6. no subway stations in my city _____

E Write the words and phrases in the correct place in the chart.

Go straight. Where is the supermarket? Is there a gym around here? The cafe is on the left.
Sorry, I don't know. ~~Turn right on Main Street.~~ Excuse me.

Get someone's attention	Ask for directions	Give directions
		Turn right on Main Street.

6 COUNTRIES

A Write the countries.

1. adnCaa _____Canada_____

2. dwneeS _____

3. kueTry _____

4. tPualrgo _____

5. nmeatiV _____

6. tliaarsuA _____

B Read the sentence. Write the nationality.

1. I'm from China. _____Chinese_____

2. Luisa is from Mexico. _____

3. Joseph is from the United States. _____

4. Nicholas is from the United Kingdom. _____

5. Ana and Sophia are from Brazil. _____

6. You are from Korea. _____

C Complete each sentence. Use *is*, *are*, *a*, or *an*.

1. It's __a__ new phone.

2. Rio de Janeiro _____ a beautiful city.

3. There _____ no buildings in the park.

4. Cristiano Ronaldo is _____ famous soccer player.

5. French is _____ interesting language.

6. It's _____ exciting theme park.

D Write the sentences. Use the words.

1. large / city / in / is / a / London / England. _____London is a large city in England._____

2. There / near / are / three / Korean / here. / restaurants _____

3. Paris. / are / parks / in / The / beautiful _____

4. country / the / Wales / United Kingdom. / in / a / is _____

5. a / There / are / China. / billion / people / in _____

6. It's / famous / a / Florida. / theme / park / in _____

E Read the questions. Write the answers.

1. What country are you from?

   _____I'm from Venezuela._____

2. What nationality are you?

   _____

3. What is your favorite food?

   _____

4. What city is beautiful?

   _____

5. Where is your neighborhood?

   _____

6. What is your country famous for?

   _____

7 FAMILY

A Write the words in the correct place in the chart.

mom   younger sister   ~~grandfather~~   mother   father   grandmother   older brother   dad

Grandparents	Parents	Children
grandfather		

B Complete the sentences.

aunt   dad   cousins   grandmother   ~~parents~~   uncle

1. My mom and dad are my _____*parents*_____.
2. My grandfather is my father's _____.
3. My mother's older sister is my _____.

4. My father's brother is my _____.
5. My aunt's mother is my _____.
6. My uncle's children are my _____.

C Write the number.

1. 22 _____*twenty-two*_____
2. 100 _____
3. 49 _____
4. 28 _____

5. 36 _____
6. 53 _____
7. 94 _____
8. 75 _____

9. 88 _____
10. 67 _____

D Complete the sentences. Use *be* or *have*.

1. My grandmother _____*is*_____ 76.
2. Our daughter _____ short hair.
3. My older brother _____ a famous actor.
4. Anita and her husband _____ a big house.

5. I _____ 22 and a student at the university.
6. She _____ my baby sister, Gabriela.
7. Jerome and Mike _____ my older brothers.
8. Dylan _____ four aunts and 12 cousins.

E Complete the chart with sentences about a family member.

Name of Family Member:	
From	
Age	
Appearance	
Job	
Family	

8 MY FAVORITES

A Write sentences. Use the words.

1. pop / a / is / singer. / sister / My / older _____ My older sister is a pop singer. _____

2. hip hop / artists. / are / famous / They _____

3. show. / popular / a / TV / is / *The Walking Dead* _____

4. friends / at / dance / are / a / club. / Our _____

5. and / sisters / My / in / a / band. / are / I / rock _____

6. watch / Japanese movies. / scary / We _____

B Write the correct form of the verb.

1. Adam (like) books. _____ likes _____

2. You (watch) TV. _____

3. My friend (read) comics. _____

4. Janet (study) English. _____

5. They (play) Bingo. _____

6. I (love) music. _____

7. My sisters (like) the singer. _____

8. Dad doesn't (know) the band. _____

9. He (watch) movies. _____

10. My parents don't (sing). _____

C Circle the correct word.

1. Tyler (like / (likes)) pop music.

2. Dad and my brother (watch / watches) soccer on TV.

3. I (read / reads) English comic books.

4. My teacher (write / writes) on the whiteboard a lot.

5. She (has / have) two pencils on her desk.

6. My older sister (love / loves) Adele's songs.

D Write the negative form of each sentence. Use *don't* or *doesn't*.

1. We like hip hop music. _____ We don't like hip hop music. _____

2. Carlos studies Japanese. _____

3. I read magazines a lot. _____

4. My cousin plays video games. _____

5. She watches funny TV shows. _____

6. You sing in a rock group. _____

E Read each sentence. Write *true* or *false* for you.

1. I don't play sports. _____ false _____

2. I'm in my classroom. _____

3. My mother's hair is short. _____

4. I sing in a rock band. _____

5. I have two older brothers. _____

6. I watch funny TV shows. _____

F Read the questions. Write answers in your notebook.

1. What is your favorite movie? _I like Star Wars._

2. What is your favorite song? _____

3. What is your favorite book? _____

4. What is your favorite TV show? _____

5. What is your favorite sport? _____

 **TIME**

A Match the times.

_c_ 1. one thirty

___ 2. ten to two

___ 3. a quarter to nine

___ 4. ten after five

___ 5. eight fifteen

___ 6. two forty-five

a. 5:10

b. 2:45

c. ~~1:30~~

d. 8:15

e. 8:45

f. 1:50

B Answer questions about the class schedule.

Morning Class Schedule	
8:00	math
8:55	science
9:50	art
10:35	break
11:00	French

Afternoon Class Schedule	
12:00	lunch
12:50	history
1:45	English
2:40	study group
3:10	P.E.

1. What time is science? _____It's at 8:55._____

2. What time is break? _____

3. What time is math? _____

4. What time is English? _____

5. What time is lunch? _____

6. What time is art? _____

C Write *true* or *false*. Use the schedule in **B**.

1. Art class is in the evening. _____false_____

2. Break is thirty-five minutes. _____

3. English starts at a quarter to two. _____

4. History is before lunch. _____

5. Science is in the afternoon. _____

6. P.E. starts at three ten. _____

D Complete the sentences. Use the words in the box.

today	in the evening	in the afternoon
after school	in the morning	~~before lunch~~

1. We have a test tomorrow morning _____before lunch_____.

2. P.E. and art are _____ after lunch.

3. Swim practice is at seven _____ before school starts.

4. Music club and band practice are _____ in the afternoon.

5. Mom watches her favorite TV show at 6:00 _____.

6. I have an appointment _____, not tomorrow.

10 MY ROUTINE

A Put the daily routines in order. Number the actions 1–5.

Morning

__1__ get up   ____ go to school

____ start school   ____ take a shower

____ have lunch

Afternoon and Evening

__1__ finish school   ____ watch TV

____ do homework   ____ go home

____ go to bed

B Complete the sentences. Use *before* or *after*.

1. I get up __before__ I check my text messages.

2. Her brother goes home _____ he finishes school.

3. I do homework _____ I go to bed.

4. Melissa takes a shower _____ she gets up.

5. In the morning, I get dressed _____ I take a shower.

6. In the evening, they watch TV _____ they go to bed.

C Write sentences. Use the words.

1. always / my / homework. / I / do _____*I always do my homework.*_____

2. eat / sometimes / at / 12:30. / lunch / We _____

3. I / early / get up / in the morning. / never _____

4. Maya and Louise / late / are / never / for / school. _____

5. We / study / often / on the weekend. / English _____

6. is / after school. / usually / Our / busy / teacher _____

D Write the sentences in the correct place in the chart.

He always goes to school before his students.	~~He often has lunch with other teachers.~~
He always does his homework.	He is sometimes nervous about tests.
He never works at the school on the weekend.	He often plays soccer with his classmates.
He usually studies with friends.	

Mr. Jackson (teacher)	Mike Smith (student)
He often has lunch with other teachers.	

E Complete the conversation. Use the words in the box.

break	homework	~~weekend~~
gym	late	work

ALEX: I'm so glad it's Friday! I need a _____.

NADIA: Yeah, me too. What do you usually do on the __weekend__, Jack?

ALEX: I get up _____. Sometimes I go shopping with my friends. How about you?

NADIA: Oh, I'm really busy. I go to the _____ on Saturday morning. Then I _____ on Saturday afternoon. On Sunday, I do _____ and go to the movies in the evening.

ALEX: Wow, you *are* busy!

11 IMPORTANT DAYS

A Write the missing months.

1. January - _____February_____ - March

2. April - May - _____

3. _____ - November - December

4. June - July - _____

5. August - _____ - October

6. February - March - _____

B Write the numbers.

1. 2nd _____second_____

2. 14th _____

3. 30th _____

4. 7th _____

5. 63rd _____

6. 32nd _____

7. 13th _____

8. 21st _____

9. 46th _____

10. 5th _____

C Match the dates.

___e__ 1. January fifth

_____ 2. September 9th

_____ 3. August third

_____ 4. March twentieth

_____ 5. December first

a. 9/9

b. 8/3

c. 12/1

d. 3/20

e. 1/5

D Write sentences. Use the words.

1. do / Where / live? / you _____Where do you live?_____

2. is / birthday? / your / When _____

3. you / Do / in the evening? / shower / a / take _____

4. you / What / do / in the morning? / do _____

5. What / on / do / you / do / weekend? / the _____

6. on / Do / have / your birthday? / a / party / you _____

E Answer the questions in **D**. Write answers that are true for you.

1. _I live in Miami, Florida._

2. _____

3. _____

4. _____

5. _____

6. _____

12 FOOD

A Write the missing letters for the foods. Then write the words on the line.

1. s _ _ p and s _ l a _   *soup and salad*
2. _ e _ e a l and _ _ u i t   _____
3. p _ s t _ or _ i _ z a   _____

4. i _ _ _ r _ a m   _____
5. s _ e _ k and _ r _ e s   _____
6. _ h i c _ e n and _ i _ e   _____

B Write the words in the correct places in the chart.

cereal	coffee	orange juice	pizza	~~soup~~	tea
chicken and rice	ice cream	pasta	soda	steak and fries	

Breakfast	Lunch or Dinner	Dessert	Drinks
	soup		

C Complete the sentences. Use the words in the box.

bag	bowl	cup	~~glass~~	piece	slice	some

1. Drink a _glass_ of water.
2. I want a _____ of pizza.
3. Eat a small _____ of soup.
4. Does your brother want a _____ of tea?

5. Do you want _____ bread?
6. Here is a _____ of popcorn.
7. Mom, can I have a _____ of pie?

D Put the conversation in the correct order.

_____ AHMED: Me. Hi, I'd like some popcorn, please.

_1_ SERVER: Who's next?

_____ SERVER: Just one bag? Large or small?

_____ AHMED: Yeah, just one small bag.

_____ AHMED: A soda, please.

_____ SERVER: Anything else with that popcorn?

_____ SERVER: OK. A small bag of popcorn and a soda. That's $3.75.

E Correct the items in the menu. There are five mistakes.

Jack's Snacks
Menu

Chicken ~~sandwish~~	$3.00	*sandwich*
Chicken taco	$2.75	_____
Stake sandwich	$3.50	_____
Pizza (slice)	$1.50	_____

Drinks

Soda	$1.25	_____
A bottle of water	$1.50	_____
A bowl of iced tea	$0.75	_____

Extras

Fries	$1.25	_____
A bowl of chips	$1.00	_____
A slice of cherry pye	$1.40	_____

E Work in a group. Play a game. Student **A** says a sentence to Student **B**.
Student **B** says a sentence to Student **C**. Say the sentence again, and again.
Student **E** says the sentence.

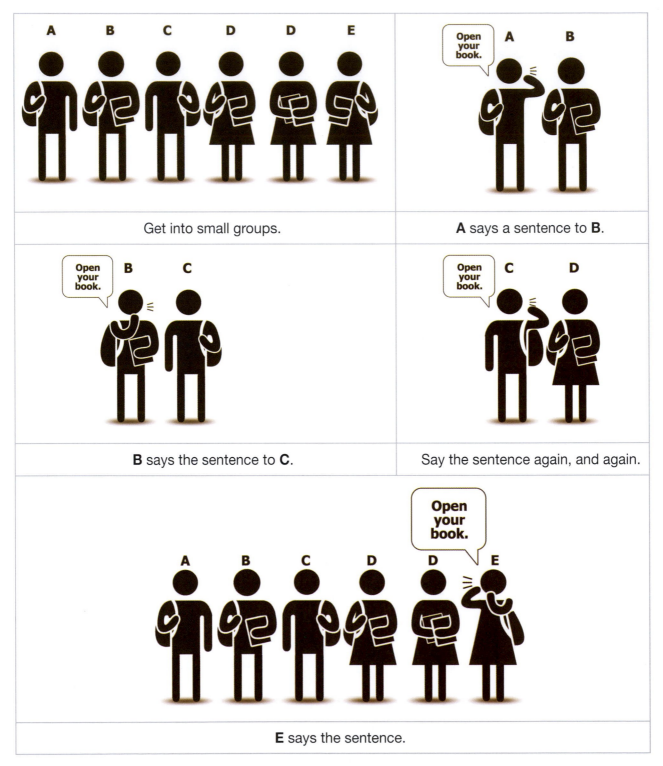

Get into small groups.

A says a sentence to **B**.

B says the sentence to **C**.

Say the sentence again, and again.

E says the sentence.

4 CROSSWORD PUZZLE

A Complete the puzzle.

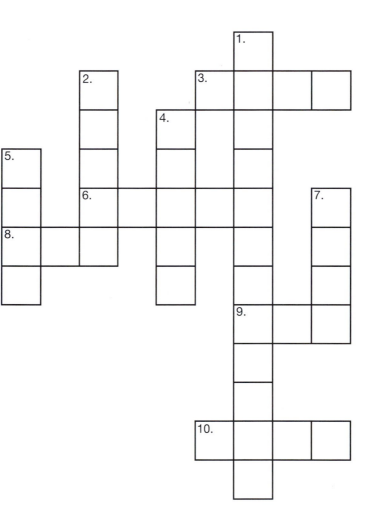

Down:

1. Listen to the _____.
2. _____ your name.
4. Can you _____ that?
5. Close _____ book.
7. Raise your _____.

Across:

3. _____ at the picture.
6. What are _____?.
8. Can I _____ your phone?
9. Listen _____ repeat.
10. Circle the _____.

B Check answers with a partner.

Student B

A Talk to your partner.

1. Ask for directions to these places. Write them on your map.

   a bus stop   an ATM
   a Chinese restaurant   a bookstore
   a drugstore   a parking garage

2. Two places above are NOT on your map. When your partner says *Sorry, I don't know*. Write an X on the words.

B Look at your map. Listen and give your partner directions. When a place is not on your map, say *Sorry, I don't know*.

Excuse me. Is there a... around here?

Yes. Go straight and...

Sorry, I don't know.

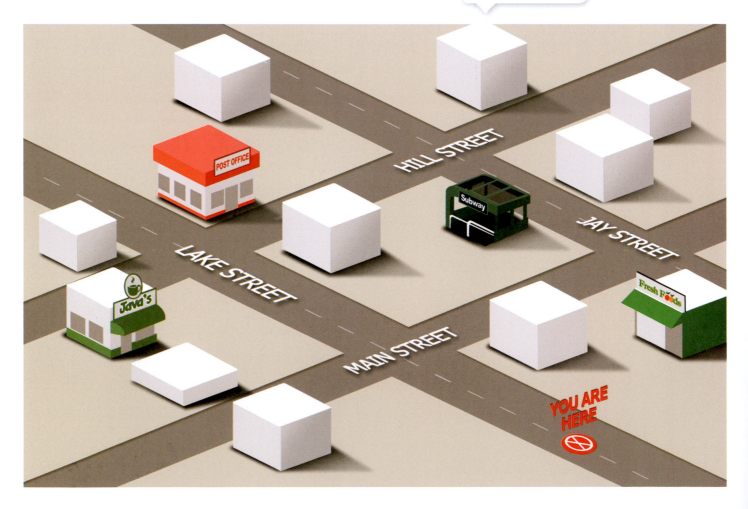

C Check answers with your partner. Are the places on your map correct?

3 ARE YOU FREE AT 2:00?

Student B

A Read your schedule silently. What activities are there? When are they?

▶ **WORD BANK**
homeroom

	Today	Tomorrow
8:00 AM		
8:45	Homeroom	Homeroom
9:00	Study group	
10:10	Science	Science
11:15		
12:00 PM	Lunch	Band practice
1:00		Lunch
2:00	English	TOEFL class
3:10	Art history	
4:10	Math	Math
5:00		
5:30		
6:00		

B You want to add the two activities below to your schedule. When are you free? Think of times.

study for your history test   go shopping

C 🔀 Your partner wants to ask you to do two activities. Listen and look at your schedule. Find a good time for both of you. Write each activity on your schedule above.

> Let's work on our science project today.

> Are you free at...?

NOTICE! ▶ You can say:
I'm free <u>at 8:00 a.m.</u>
<u>before school</u>.
<u>in the morning</u>.

> Sounds good. When?

> No. I have.... I'm free...

D 🔀 Ask your partner to do the two activities in **B**. Find a good time for both of you. Then write the activities on your schedule above.

Unit 1

answer (the question)

ask (your teacher)

circle (the word)

close (your book)

cover (the page)

listen (and repeat)

look at (the picture)

open (your book)

read (the sentence)

say (the word)

write (your name)

yes

no

please

numbers 1–5

Unit 2

businessman/woman

doctor

programmer

soccer player

student

teacher

Mr. / Ms.

Unit 3

backpack

(white)board

bookcase

chair

clock

(laptop) computer

desk

dictionary

door

eraser

map

notebook

pen

pencil

phone

screen

table

textbook

umbrella

window

ID card

Put it Together 1

I don't know.

Unit 4

zero

one

two

three

four

five

six

seven

eight

nine

ten

eleven

twelve

thirteen

fourteen

fifteen

sixteen

seventeen

eighteen

nineteen

twenty

student ID number

email address

phone number

@ = at

.com = dot com

.edu = dot e-d-u

.net = dot net

(best) friend

different

new

Sorry!

Yeah.

Unit 5

neighborhood

ATM

bank

bus stop

cafe / coffee shop

gym

movie theater

park

post office

restaurant

school

store

supermarket

car

garage

tree

bookstore

clothing store

department store

favorite

street